We all experience the betrayal of others, the disappointment of making poor decisions, and the desire to finally be assured that in spite of our past missteps and current sense of brokenness, we are enough. In *Junk to Jewels,* Georgette Beck reminds us that God is still God, our lives still have value, and the best is still yet come.

—JOHN O'LEARY,
National best selling author of the books *In Awe* and *On Fire.*

Georgette Beck's new book, *Junk to Jewels,* is a brave, honest, and vulnerable gift of hope and comfort to anyone journeying through their own ashes-to-beauty story. Georgette's heart for the hurting and hope for the healing is in every word and palpable from cover to cover. I have the pleasure of Georgette's friendship, first meeting at a writer/speaker conference in 2015. Her character is deeply rooted in Christ-centered goodness and generosity, and I believe that, as you read *Junk to Jewels,* you will find that she will become your friend as well. I am better for having Georgette in my life and reading her work of heart, *Junk to Jewels.* I believe the same will be true for you.

—ANDREA STUNZ,
Editor + Writer + Growth Coach + Beauty Hunter (AndreaStunz.com)

This is an author's first published book. I was privileged to read this when it was only a rough draft, but I overwhelmingly applaud this first book by Georgette Beck. I hope you have the opportunity to read and enjoy this book. I think you will at times both laugh and cry. You will certainly be inspired to pursue a deeper, more meaningful relationship with God and to search for your own greater purpose in life.

In the book, Ms. Beck describes her journey of raising her young daughter as a single parent while recovering from a heart wrenching divorce. There are poignant descriptions of her sadness but also of her extreme joy as she moves through many hardships and challenges toward finding the love of her life and soulmate. During the journey, she also discovers more about her own life, relationship with God, and her purpose on this earth. I highly recommend and appreciate this great literary project Ms. Beck has created to give inspiration and motivation to others. It comes from someone who has genuinely shared a deep part of her heart and passion with us as readers. Looking forward to what Ms. Beck has in store for us next!

—JOANNIE COUNCILLOR,
Realtor

Junk to Jewels is a riveting journey that highlights blessings from above, initially disguised as difficulties. As each path unfolded, I naturally began to reflect upon the gems in my own life that once started off as seemingly hopeless circumstances. Every chapter was a reminder that junk cannot exist when you walk with God and that miracles can happen when a prayer is cried out. What a delightful reinforcement that faith (not fear) and gratitude (not grudges) will pave your way to tender joy and precious jewels!

—LAURA BURGESS
Owner and Master Coach - Meet The Future

Georgette Beck shares her life experiences in an authentic and vulnerable narrative in which she writes with a sincere desire to help others know their worth. Her testimony helps her readers know to look to God for guidance and will inspire them to press forward, with faith, to achieve their dreams.

—LARA DONNELL

a journey from
brokenness & despair to
beauty & delight

JUNK
TO
JEWELS

Georgette Beck

Fedd Books
P.O. Box 341973
Austin, TX 78734
www.thefeddagency.com

Published in association with The Fedd Agency, Inc., a literary agency.

Cover Design: Christian Rafetto (www.humblebooksmedia.com)

ISBN: 978-1-964508-15-3

LCCN: 2024902628

Printed in the United States of America

TABLE OF CONTENTS

DEDICATION

Jessica, you are my "sweet, precious opal," a gift and a blessing to me. I love you, and I am proud of you. May your gems shine brilliantly as you impact our world for good.

Mom, you are forever and always within me, gorgeous and talented, a writer yourself. I will forever be grateful for your creative gifts and love of reading, which you have passed on to me. I love you.

Foreword

In a world marred by brokenness and pain, the journey of Georgette stands as a testament to the transformative power of God's grace. Within the pages of this book, you will encounter a narrative of rejection, divorce, and regeneration—a story not of despair, but of hope and redemption. Through the lens of faith and perseverance, as her journey unfolds, revealing the profound truth that even in our darkest moments, God's hand is ever-present, guiding us toward healing and restoration.

As you immerse yourself in these pages, prepare to be inspired by the resilience of the human spirit and the unfailing love of our Creator. Through the trials and tribulations faced by Georgette, you will witness firsthand the miraculous ways in which God works in the lives of those who trust in Him. From the depths of despair to the heights of spiritual renewal, this narrative serves as a beacon of hope for anyone who has ever felt cast aside or alone.

Ultimately, this book is a celebration of God's faithfulness and the re-markable journey of self-discovery and transformation that unfolds when we surrender our lives to His divine plan. I have known her as a friend and Pastor for many years and have been encouraged by Georgette's journey and growth. I know she hopes this will serve as a source of encouragement and inspiration for all who dare to believe that, with God's help, no trial is too great to overcome and no brokenness beyond repair. As you embark on this journey of faith and renewal, may you be reminded that, in the hands of a powerful God, there is always hope for a brighter tomorrow.

—LLOYD HEILMAN, M.D., M.Div.

SECTION I

The Rescue

Even to your old age and gray hairs I am he, I am
he who will sustain you. I have made you and I will
carry you; I will sustain you and I will rescue you.

—ISAIAH 46:4 (NIV)

CHAPTER 1
Living Death

"Death is the prerequisite to resurrection, the new life God intends."

—JOHN ORTBERG

"I want a divorce!"

I wonder how many other couples say these words to each other. Maybe even on a daily basis, carelessly yelling the words to their partner in desperation as a threat. It was my go-to tool when I felt unheard or urgently wanted my husband to pay attention and listen to me. I learned from experience that this tool boomerangs.

I loved my husband, and for this story, let's call him Damien. Even when our marriage was painful and difficult, I never desired a divorce. When I used the word "divorce," my heart didn't really want it. But sadly, *divorce* was threatened too many times and eventually came to fruition.

While I used the word, hoping my spouse would understand he should be taking my conversation with him seriously, one day, he responded in ways my heart never wanted. He agreed. He embraced the word for himself. One day, one of us used the word and meant it.

Dr. Willard Harley explains his love bank concept by describing how two people fall and stay in love. We had not been making enough deposits

3

of kind words, actions, or enjoyable experiences with each other, only withdrawals, hurtful words, and not enough quality time together. Our love banks were continually empty and in the red zone.

Of course, he and I paid attention to them at first. The day I came home from my hair appointment after I had a male beautician wash, cut, and style my hair was one of them. I cried uncontrollably the whole way home. The gentle touches set something off within me; they stirred deep and unfulfilled yearnings. I was starving for love in the ways I needed to receive love. That episode moved us to seek out counseling, and it helped a bit, but for us, it just became a band-aid to cover the real problems. The love bank stayed empty. The red zone got darker.

Damien and I were arguing about his working all the time and not spending much time with me. Loneliness within marriage is no joke, and ours was not a healthy marriage for multiple reasons. When things are out of balance, the little problems become big problems, and everything becomes dysfunctional.

The day my husband agreed to my desperate threat, the argument turned into a pleading session, with me getting down on my knees, crying as if my life depended on it. No matter what I said or how much I cried, nothing changed his mind. The argument was over when he walked out of the house.

It was over. It truly was. I cried out, "Oh God, what do I do?"

I walked upstairs and found myself in my walk-in closet, looking around at all my personal belongings. My mind was racing, replaying the scene in the kitchen over and over. I would have to face it: my marriage was over. The pain that had been stuffed down throughout the years had boiled over. Deep cries from the depths of my soul overtook me.

As I cried on the floor, I noticed my floral, heart-shaped box in the corner of the closet, holding every card Damien and I had given to each other throughout the past decade. I took the lid off and reached for the top card. It was so pretty. I opened it and saw the handwriting. I always liked how he formed his letters and signed his name. I read his words to me. He had a gift for picking out sweet cards. I reached for the next one and then the next, reading until the box was empty. I gently put the whole pile of cards back into my heart-shaped box. The contents held the written proof of our love for each other. Also evident were the reoccurring words, "I'm sorry."

I lay down and curled into a fetal position. The tears seemed endless.

I thought about our life, the one we'd created together, as I looked around the closet. We had a beautiful home on a gorgeous corner wooded lot overlooking a lovely brook. Guilford, Connecticut, was a beautiful country town with prime public schools—a deciding factor for us as to where we would live since our daughter would soon enter kindergarten. I knew we'd planned well in ensuring our daughter was in a place where she would receive a good education. I suppose we should have planned better for her to have a good family.

"I don't want a divorce! Please don't leave!"

It was like he hadn't even heard me. He ignored me, but this was nothing new. I was invisible. Wasn't I always?

Our marriage was a mess from the beginning. One of the things that attracted me to Damien was his love for his family, but ironically, it's the one thing that undermined our marriage the most. We were never able to live independent lives from his family. They weren't accepting of outsiders, nor did they wish to allow one of their members to leave the fold, especially to leave the nest for marriage at such a young age. This was a generational repeat on my part; history was repeating itself.

My parents had also married young, and the make-up of my dad's family of origin was identical to my husband's, with a sister and brothers.

As sons, they were both responsible for helping their families with financial support. My dad and Damien were both landscapers and workaholics with the same level of education.

"God, please help me," I remember crying out. I was alone in my heart, alone in my soul, and alone on the floor of my dream home's bedroom closet.

We were Christians. Christians don't just give up on their marriage and walk away, especially if children are involved. What about our daughter? Did he not care about her? What about the life we had planned together? What would happen to us?

I had no family here, and his family hadn't wanted him to marry me. When he wanted to propose to me during the summer around my birthday, his family convinced him to delay the proposal and create a hope chest to gift instead. He built it himself using cedar wood. It was to place household items in for our future. Over the next year, I filled it with a blanket and several cute knickknacks I envisioned decorating our first home with. Come Christmas time, he did propose, but with no great support from his family. I was only eighteen, and they felt we were too young. My family was ecstatic. We had been dating for almost three years at that point. We loved each.

On the floor of my closet, I continued beseeching God. I wailed. I bawled. I whimpered, pled, and prayed. I begged and sobbed, then nothing but stillness. My head throbbed, and my chest ached. Was this what death felt like? I had wondered if God heard me.

Without my permission, the scene from the kitchen played out repeatedly in my mind in explicit detail. But at some point, I was an observer, not a participant, almost like watching a movie.

"Mommy?"

I snapped out of my detached mental state. I was not dreaming. The conversation happened. Damien was gone. My daughter called for me, and I couldn't let her find me here.

My body responded, knowing what to do. Thank goodness because the rest of me sure didn't.

I mentioned before about the warning signs. Throughout our dating, the "red flags" went unnoticed, not understood, or maybe purposely ignored. Hindsight truly is 20/20. The night before our wedding rehearsal dinner, even a glaring sign could not save me. While moving into our new home, my fiancé confessed to going to a strip joint with his older brother, who "forced" him. Yes, you heard me correctly. This brother forced my 6'2" fiancé into a strip club and kept him there for hours. What a feat. I was devastated, crying my heart out on Damien's lap in our newly received rocking chair. Did I hold him accountable? No. I didn't even know how to do that. I blamed the brother, of course.

My husband eventually returned after the argument in the kitchen, where he'd left me on my knees, begging him not to go. But he did not change his mind about the divorce. Fear overtook my heart and became a full-time resident. Each day brought no hope. I somehow made it to work. I barely made it home when I went out at night. The husband, who now hated me, was in the house with me. He would still be gone, working all the time but would come home, though I never knew when that would be.

Divorce feels like a living death. The painful reality becomes clear when one of the two-become-one pair decides to end things. Anxiety and fear were constant, and depression soon joined.

People self-medicate in different ways. For me, alcohol was my choice. It instantly made me feel better, though I would later realize the actual effects of alcohol. For starters, it intensifies the effects of depression, something my already big emotions did not need help with.

The party in my heart and mind gained momentum. Despair settled in uninvited. I had no idea what was going to happen. I was scared.

🪨 JEWELS ⬤

I hope you hear me when I say that after the death comes the resurrection. Loss lingers, but hope arises. Through despair, we ever-so-gently find our footing, as guided by God's great love. Diamonds are created by way of intense pressure. Sorrow becomes joy. "You have turned for me my mourning into dancing; You have loosed my sackcloth and girded me with gladness" (Psalm 30:11 NAS).

Dear one, you may be depressed, in despair, and surrounded by darkness. Your rescue can begin here—a rescue to deliver, safeguard, redeem, and protect you from harm. Your liberation, release, and recovery will come.

Maybe your brokenness is from the loss of a valued relationship or a job you enjoyed. Maybe your despair is from heart wounds you carry that have never been addressed or healed. Whatever the circumstances or however you are feeling, you are someone who matters. You have significance, and situations do not remain the same forever. You can choose to change. Changing yourself and your perspective changes everything.

New insight shifts perspective. You may be one shift away from your new beginning. Brian Tracy, a motivational speaker and self-development author, has said, "You cannot control what happens to you, but you can control your attitude toward what happens to you, and in that, you will be mastering change rather than allowing it to master you."

May courage guide you to pray and ask God for His help! Cry out for your rescue. And remember, never threaten the end of something if you do not mean it. Victim or Victor? The choice is ours. Hugh Prather said,

"One says, 'I am powerless over my inner demons' and gives in to them. The other makes the same admission and asks for help."

When everything falls apart, this is the time to invite your trusted loved ones to be around you and to put in place valuable, helpful tools and strategies to provide urgently needed support as you gather all of the broken pieces to gently place them softly on the shelves of your heart to be there for you when you are able to work through the facts of what has occurred. Not all fear is bad. Fear tells us something is not right and may not be safe. Protect your heart and emotions now. Learn to distinguish between helpful fears and imposter fears. Face each fear.

Joyce Meyer reminds us that "Suffering and tragedy are part of life. The Bible even tells us we will suffer and encounter trials, so we must learn how to deal with them in ways that help us overcome them instead of letting them overcome us" (*Never Give Up).* The journey through life encompasses mountaintops and valleys. Rest assured, if you have never experienced a loss or crisis, you will. The good news is that you do have options on how to respond. You may or may not have control over the circumstances, but your response is something always within your control. You do not have to remain stuck in despair, and you do not have to let a crisis, whether temporary or long-term, rob you of living a healthy, joy-filled life. You may hit bottom, but staying there is optional. You can bounce back up toward becoming whole again, but this has its own timetable. Heading in the right direction where your freedom can be found is your success, one breath at a time. Remember, it bears repeating: if you have no control of circumstances or someone else's actions, you absolutely DO have control of yourself. Joyce Meyer said, "Whatever you find yourself in the middle of, determine to see it all the way through to the finish."

And golly gee, would you seriously consider never using the "divorce" word as a threat in your marriage or threatening to end your committed relationship, unless, of course, this is exactly what you wish for yourself? Our thoughts and words *do* dictate our future.

Decide not to spiral. God already has you and is waiting for your call for help, and His hand will take your hand to begin a new journey down a new path together. He desires a glorious life for you. Don't settle for less. You have an enemy of the soul who desires destruction for you. There is a precious jewel within you, and God desires the best for you and plans to uncover every single sparkle. This pain—this season—will not last.

> *If you are distressed by anything external, the pain is not due to the thing itself, but to your estimate of it; and this you have the power to revoke at any moment.*
>
> **—MARCUS AURELIUS**

CHAPTER 2
The Rescue

"God has lifted me out of the horrible pit, and He set my feet upon a rock and put a new song in my mouth."

—PSALM 40:2-3

Light began to shine in the darkness. God came to me, even if I didn't notice.

"How gracious he will be when you cry for help! As soon as he hears, he will answer you" (Isaiah 30:19 NIV).

"Then you will call upon me and come and pray to me, and I will listen to you" (Jeremiah 29:12 NIV).

"You will pray to him, and he will hear you" (Job 22:27 NIV).

"Then you will call, and the Lord will answer; you will cry for help, and he will say: Here am I" (Isaiah 58:9 NIV).

"He will call upon me, and I will answer him" (Psalm 91:15 NIV).

God heard my heart cries from the closet floor—in the home that was supposed to be the "dream home." His rescue began. He raises the poor from the dust and lifts the needy from the ash heap (Psalm 113:7). God was everywhere, helping me. I may not have noticed initially, but slowly, ever-so-gently, I realized His touches and interventions.

The first person God used was someone I would not have expected. My husband's sister stopped by the house and gave me a music CD, the "Preacher's Wife" soundtrack. Each song I listened to felt like God's healing words sung over my broken heart. I wore that CD out. I often sat in my car and listened to the songs on repeat, the lyrics planting seeds of hope. My sister-in-law was the first heart God used to provide a lifeline of His Words directly to my heart. I loved my sister-in-law from the onset. I admired her and emulated her. I would wear the perfumes she wore and purchase Dooney & Burke purses, just like she did. But throughout the years, it had seemed to me on many occasions that she was avoiding me and had time to have a relationship with her brother but not with me. She had cried all day on our wedding day, and I truly believed she may have been glad our marriage was ending—that she would be glad to have her brother back. But my thinking was based on an extremely insecure self. I had unfair expectations for what our relationship should look like because I desired to be loved and favored like my husband was. I wanted this for myself, too, and my need for acceptance and belonging caused me to believe and behave in unhealthy ways. Many of my insecurities were tied to my perception of rejection. Beth Moore describes how it is entirely possible to perceive a rejection when we haven't been rejected. "We might have wanted *all* the attention of someone who was only willing to give us a significant portion. We may, for instance, want to be treated as the favorite child of a parent of two or a stepparent of four. Or we may want to be the only friend of *our* friend. Or we may want to be the absolute apex of our man's attention, and when we don't get what we crave in the relationship we've exalted, we feel rejected. We can confuse 80 percent reciprocation with 100 percent rejection" (*So Long Insecurity*). This sums up my childhood feelings, my marriage feelings, and my perception as to how I was accepted or not accepted by my in-laws.

All these years later, I remain humbled by how and who God used to speak love to my heart when I felt so alone and so unlovable.

My parents seemed to understand the seriousness of our situation and decided to leave their sunny Florida oasis and come to Connecticut for Christmas. Many circumstances would prove God's faithfulness in unbelievable ways, and their visit was just the beginning. God stabilized our home and marriage at the critical juncture of signing a new lease to move my daughter and myself into a condominium with a loft. The loft, wide open with no walls and steep stairs, was where my five-year-old would sleep. Not the safest logistic for a little girl. My head was not in a good place, and I was clearly not thinking straight (but my husband had no issue with this tentative moving out plan). My parents' visit brought light and hope, encouraging a change in my husband's heart. Damien decided to give our marriage another chance if we moved to Florida.

God orchestrated the whole move from Connecticut to Florida, His rescue mission beginning with an immediate uprooting. I resigned from my career of seven years, an organization I had loved. When the branch manager asked why I was leaving, I replied, "I wanted to give my marriage everything I have, to know that I did give everything to help save it." They all thought I was making a mistake. I was valued there.

Divine interventions and miracles continued.

God placed us in just the right community and neighborhood.

Education is of utmost importance to me, and having Jessica in a choice school was a priority. She had to finish her kindergarten year at a school far away via a bus (scary for this momma). The first day I waited for her at the bus stop at the end of school, the bus was late. I had never had to entrust my baby in this way. After I observed her teacher screaming at the children, I made a point to be present and involved. Our prayers deepened for a Christian school, and through a series of God's divine appointments, we discovered the perfect private Christian school, Morningside Academy. The office was peaceful, and the staff was super friendly. It felt like home. Jessica was enrolled and accepted. To say my heart was relieved would have been an understatement. This school connected to a church, so we began attending worship services there.

One Sunday, I saw in the church bulletin a notice that Crisis Pregnancy Services (now CareNet) was looking for an administrative assistant. I applied for the position and was offered the job. I was surrounded by Christians, women who immediately took me under their wing. This environment added to the seeds planted in my heart for starting my future ministry, Bella Healing Hearts Foundation.

One morning, my new boss told me that the church would start a new women's Bible study, and she thought I should participate. The group would meet at the facilitator's home, and all the ladies attending would meet in our church parking lot to carpool. Her home, if you can call it that, was on Hutchinson Island. We got off the elevator, which opened directly into her penthouse suite, and all you saw was grandeur and beauty. There were wondrous views of the Atlantic Ocean everywhere you looked. The penthouse was luxurious, spacious, and finely designed with quality furnishings with gold decor and art hanging on the walls. We were all astounded. I felt like royalty and have never experienced such beauty. It was Heaven on earth. Our weekly studies together became such a heart and spiritual treat. Love flowed generously. I met my new spiritual mommas, Margaret Ruplin and Joyce Hietala, and other strong Christian women of faith. Powerful things happened in our little group of women. Miss Margaret and Joyce shepherded us girls for years to come. Joyce even had her own special morning fax ministry. She would fax all the girls a daily page with various scriptures, personal faith reminders for us to reflect on, and even cute witty statements or quotes. These became the highlight of my day, and I referred to them often. These were some of my favorites.

"It's not your outlook but your 'up look' that counts" (Psalm 123:2).

"If you put forth a smile, one will usually find its way back."

"A day hemmed in prayer is less likely to unravel" (Philemon 4:6,7).

"He who jumps to conclusions cannot always expect a happy landing."

"If you want peace of mind, don't give anyone a piece of yours."

God continually brought me into situations and to people that kept me going. They were lifelines and circumstances that provided spiritual teaching and training. Jessica and I were embraced by father, mother, sister, and brother figures. In the beginning, my husband attended church with us, but over time his participation lessened and eventually stopped. God used everything and everyone to help me heal, to help me understand where I had come from and what had happened from His perspective. God showed me how I could come to like myself, to learn who I was in His eyes. He showed me the beauty of me.

My husband became angry and unforgiving. It hurt. His commitment to our marriage wavered. He expressed that he did not love me anymore and no longer desired to be married to me. The problems were "all my fault." I believed this in the beginning until God showed me the truth.

🪨 JEWELS 🪙

God will always respond to your cries for help in creative, unique ways. God is your strength in times of trouble (Psalm 37:39 NLV). The Lord is good and a safe place in times of trouble (Nahum 1:7 NLV). He is your hiding place where you are kept safe from trouble (Psalm 32:7 NLV). God will make you strong again after your troubles (Psalm 71:20 NLV). The Lord is your strength and safe cover; you are helped (Psalm 28:7 NLV). The Lord is your rock, your safe place, and the One who takes you out of trouble and is your safe covering, saving strength, and strong tower (Psalm 18:2 NLV).

Admitting to yourself the truth of your state of mind, heart, and life is the first step. Let go of distractions or negative people or places that may hinder your progress. You can turn your failures into triumphs.

"Like the alcoholic, you have to face what your defense is costing you," said Matthew McKay and Patrick Fanning. Your expectations may be flawed from flawed thinking. They suggest "disarming the critic" because when you judge yourself harshly, nearly every aspect of life becomes more difficult. Here are some examples:

- It's hard to be open or revealing with people because you expect them to reject "the real you."

- You get very angry or depressed when criticized.

- You avoid social situations where there is a chance of criticism or rejection. You don't take risks; you don't meet new people, and you endure loneliness rather than reach out.

- You avoid challenges because you expect to fail.

- It's hard to say no or set limits in relationships because you would feel wrong if the other person got upset.

Your self-esteem has taken a hit and is fragile, or maybe it was already nonexistent. The good news is there are proven cognitive techniques for improving and maintaining your self-esteem. God's scriptures are the most powerful transformative approach you can utilize. His Word speaks truth, and when you speak these out loud to yourself, you speak life into yourself.

"I've been heartbroken. I've broken hearts. That's part of life, and it's part of figuring out who you are so you can find the right partner."

—HEIDI KLUM

CHAPTER 3
Edge of Hell

"She believed that the damage to her mind and heart was permanent, until she met wisdom, who taught her that no pain or wound is eternal, that all can be healed, and that love can grow even in the toughest parts of her being."

—YUNG PUEBLO

If there was life in me, I didn't recognize it. I was in daily conversation with God, mainly through my tears. I also began consistently journaling again. Through those pages, my prayers and relationship with God came alive.

During that period of my spiritual growth, Damien had read about an upcoming mission trip to Haiti in the church bulletin and expressed interest. While I wouldn't be able to go, his interest in going had given me hope for our marriage. I believed this would provide circumstances for Damien to experience a divine touch from God through other Christians and through serving others in need. I prayed he would get to go!

I made every effort to consider Damien's needs—to make him feel important. Instead of complaining that he was never home, I'd been convicted by God to start waking up early to make him lunch. God also moved on my heart to seek forgiveness and extend it to other family members by writing letters. I was working on relationship healing. During one of my

Bible study meetings, during prayer, Joyce had a vision about Damien. She saw two large angels standing behind Damien, approximately 7' tall, rugged looking. One of the angels had his finger on Damien's heart. I shared this vision with Damien later that evening, and we ended up having a lovely night together. The next day, I was pleasantly surprised when Damien had a gift for me in a pretty box with a red bow. Inside the box was a sexy red lingerie outfit with stockings and a bottle of massage lotion. I was hopeful for more intimacy between us.

For my birthday, I was with our Bible study girls. They invited me to share my testimony. The girls showered me with cards and gifts, and I felt so loved. Joyce prayed scripture over me: "As for me, this is my promise to them, says the Lord, my Holy Spirit shall not leave them, and they shall want the good and hate the wrong, they and their children and their children's children forever" (Isaiah 59:21 TLB). Joyce prayed that my words would not come from my emotions, but from my heart, and to put a zipper on my lips. Miss Margaret also shared scripture for my birthday: "So don't worry about these things, saying, 'What will we eat? What will we drink? What will we wear?' These things dominate the thoughts of unbelievers, but your heavenly Father already knows all your needs. Seek the Kingdom of God above all else, and live righteously, and He will give you everything you need" (Matthew 6:31-33 NLT).

Damien and I had another argument. Joyce's prayer over me the Tuesday night before went right out the window. Damien blurted, out of the blue, that he was going to get a vasectomy. *Take a knife and just stab it through my heart already.*

"You will not live here anymore," I voiced my emotions. As soon as I said it, I felt scared. I didn't want him not to live here anymore. But why was he doing this? Was his verbal and emotional abuse not enough already? Wasn't he telling me by his words and actions that he wanted out? Now, he was looking for a way for me to be the one to kick him out. He wanted someone else to take the fall for his cowardice.

I told him all of this and more during our argument. He did not have the right to decide that there would be no more children in our future, for our family and me. It was crazy that he would have the nerve to go through an operation that, from what others have said, is a very painful experience. Yet, he couldn't muster enough courage to work on some of the tough issues that brought us here. This was too bold of a sign for me. His getting a vasectomy, in a way, would signify the death of our relationship. I could not believe how hard he was trying to hurt and push me away. I would never be able to change enough for his liking. But I realized that's not even what he wanted. He didn't want to change, and he didn't want me to change either. If I changed, it wouldn't give him an excuse to leave. If I stayed horrible, if I was the one who kicked him out, he could live with himself. That was his reason for wanting to go through with this procedure.

The next morning, Damien dropped another bomb, "I'm not going to Haiti."

I'm not sure what I said. I hung up the phone in shock.

I called Miss Margaret in tears. She took time to speak to me and to pray for me. She wisely counseled, "Georgette, you need to step back. Damien is the leader, the head. You have already shared your feelings. God knows your heart. You need to allow God to take control and handle things. You need to let God fight this battle."

Her words and prayers brought me before God with my own prayers. I cried and poured out my hurts and hopes to God. Later, when Damien called, I was ready.

"So, what's up? Are you leaving me? Are you going to kick me out?" Damien asked.

I replied, "Damien, no, I am not leaving you or kicking you out. I will tell you again: I disagree with you on this matter. Your decision to go through this procedure hurts me. We may decide not to have any more kids, but if you go through this operation, we won't have any choice in this area. It is forever. This was not what God intended for married people. I will not try to control you. You are the head of our marriage. This is sad for me, but it's your decision to make. And it's your decision on whether you go to Haiti."

The call ended. My heart was all over the place. I had a feeling that wasn't how he'd wanted it to go. Maybe he was prepared for more of a fight. I wasn't sure I could survive if he chose to keep us from having more children.

We had a rough couple of weeks. I put my entire focus on Damien and our situation. I felt alone, unloved, and uncared for. I was incredibly lonely. Damien was distant and detached and offered no words of encouragement. He offered nothing. My prayers were non-stop. I also prayed with Miss Margaret and other Christians. I asked God to please help me obey His Word and love Damien no matter the circumstances. The pain was unbearable. I remembered how I felt when I got married. I was happy, in love, and loved! Nothing like the crushing sadness I felt now.

One month turned into another and then another. Damien and I were up and down like a brutal roller coaster ride. I continually sought prayer from the women in my life, but things at home didn't improve. The Haiti mission trip came up a few times. He was going. He wasn't going. I suffered from all the back and forth, the uncertainty. I don't know if Damien followed through with the vasectomy, but he did go on the mission trip. I would later discover how that trip sealed the fate of our marriage. Thankfully, I was able to keep my focus on God. I had nowhere else to turn, no one else to turn to. Besides, I had other issues to deal with—like the broken relationship with my parents.

God, please keep helping me. I need your help. Tomorrow night, I plan on attending an Adult Children of Alcoholics meeting. I can do all things through Christ Jesus. I will be OK. I will not be anxious about tomorrow. God, you are taking care of me. I will do my part. Please help me with the rest.

Entering that recovery meeting taught me more about myself and shed additional light on growing up with my parents. This greater understanding of myself and why I did what I did was eye-opening. It breathed fresh new life into my mind, heart, and soul. I was able to forgive myself and to have mercy toward myself and others. I knew further amends would need to be made, however. What a mess it all was.

I spoke to my father-in-law, apologizing for the "wall" I had up and for some of the things I did. I explained some of the "whys" with the tools I learned in the meetings. What I remember about this emotional conversation was that I shared how hurt I had been when their support for our decision to marry was not evident, by the unrealistic expectation that we had to attend every single family gathering, and that their phone calls that consumed much of Damien's time at night after he'd worked all day were hurtful to our marriage. He did not realize the extent of how their possessiveness of their son's time had robbed me of spending time with my husband. I also shared how sorry I was for having been so needy and controlling of my husband's time and overprotective of our daughter. They loved me, and their son and forgave me as I forgave them. Matters with my own family hadn't improved.

It had seemed as if my own family loved my husband more than me. They blamed me for the breakdown of our marriage and the tentative upcoming separation and divorce. They told me no matter what, my husband was always welcome at family gatherings. Of course, I was still hoping with all my heart Damien would change his mind about his plans to move out that seemed to be forever on the horizon. I knew he was struggling with his decision, which is why I believe he seemed to want me to be the one to ask him to leave. The guilt weighed heavy. I'm sure neither of us wanted to be that person who ultimately ended the marriage. He kept going back and forth on trying to forgive me and saying his heart was in the marriage, and then he'd change his mind and decide he no longer wished to be married to me.

My sister made plans to go to the comedy club with him.

My sister and her husband let him rent one of their rooms for a while.

My sister even gifted me figurines that were originally mine and my husband's, but unbeknownst to me, he had taken them from our home and told her not to let me know he had given them to her.

My family had planned a weekend trip with my husband and daughter, but my mother later canceled it because she felt guilty for leaving me behind.

Dennis Rainey's book, *The Tribute,* came across my path. Gary Smalley's words on the cover moved me enough to purchase the book. "In a generation where parent-bashing has become the norm, Dennis Rainey shows us a tangible way to acknowledge, thank, and honor our parents for what they did right." Wow, how true.

We know our parents may have messed things up for themselves or their children, but how often do we honor them for the many things they may have done right? God had me on a path of forgiveness and making amends. I knew He wanted me to gain additional insight into parenting in general, about my parents and myself. I needed to show humility toward others, especially those I felt had hurt me. Whether they were aware of the hurt they had caused or not, extending humility to those around you can move mountains.

I took Mr. Rainey's advice to heart and felt God leading me to write tributes to my parents and siblings. I wrote something for each of them and framed each to read to them on Thanksgiving Day. This would be the perfect time to remind each of them how much I love them and what wonderful memories I treasure about each of them. I told them how special they were. It was a beautiful moment.

He was there, since my parents had made it clear that Damien was welcome at all family gatherings. But we did not talk to each other. If we exchanged a hello or goodbye, that was about it. I was thankful he was there to see the restoration in my heart and my family. Maybe he would have a change of heart toward me and wish to save our marriage. My heart remained ignorant to his words and actions portraying otherwise.

A few days later, Damien reminded me that he planned to move out after Christmas. He still had no desire to be with me anymore. I noticed the sun shining as I was on my way to work. The contrast between the sunshine and the clouds in my spirit was obvious. I made it to work with swollen eyes and a broken heart.

December of 1997 brought the holiday season, usually my favorite season. That year, however, I remember not wanting to wake up, wishing my mattress would absorb me. My daughter was crying in her sleep again. The tree went up the day before, and we decorated it. Damien put the lights on it and put lights in Jessie's bathroom, then left for the whole night.

The next day, as I headed out to pick up Jessica from school, Greg, our apartment manager, drove by in his truck. "You are changing. You look good," he said.

I smiled and said, "Thank you!" His kind words felt good to me and filled a bit of a longing to be seen in a positive manner, to feel pretty. I hoped I was changing for the better—emotionally, spiritually, and physically. I still felt like a loser, like I wasn't healthy or worthy enough for someone to like me. I wanted to be seen differently, to be different, to be a different person—a more confident, loved person.

* * *

Limbo. Oblivion. Nothingness, nowhere, and out there—this is where I found myself. The land of limbo is a strange place to exist. It feels like you take one step forward and three steps back. While there, it was imperative to be surrounded by trusted, healthy support. I also coped by staying busy—for Jessie and me.

I learned a critical lesson: if your partner is not living with you or committed to your relationship, do not sleep with them. I walked through the pain of being available whenever my husband showed up—which was usually late at night. Head games, heart games; it was all a nasty business.

On the first day of my "separated" life, February 7, 1998, I realized that I had never lived alone. I cried when Damien was about to go. He hugged me for a while, and it felt kind. I had a hard time letting go.

I remember calling him just after midnight. We had the most intimate conversation we'd ever had with each other.

"I care about you and love you," he shared. "I will always take care of you."

We talked until almost 3:00 a.m., laughing and crying.

Damien called me in the morning to see if I had woken up. He picked up Jessica from school that day—they were outside riding bikes when I got home. We all came in, and Damien and I hugged for the longest time and kissed a little too. He was tender and emotional, with tears in his eyes.

"Do you hate me?" he asked.

"No, I could never," I said. "I love, love, love you. I even like you!"

A new neighbor below my apartment had started paying special attention to me. He came over to watch a movie, and I felt things I hadn't felt in years. Those feelings scared me, but it felt good to have someone desire me and to be held and touched. I didn't let things progress fully, not as much as I wanted them to. Many spiritual things were happening within me at this time. My fear of not being right with God and feeling so messed up overwhelmed me. Fear of abandonment and rejection was realized. Understanding how lonely I had been for far too long shed light on my level of emptiness, vulnerability, and need for affection. Beth Moore tells us, "Nothing shouts a more convincing lie about our personal value than rejection, and it can reverberate with deafening pitch from any direction."

Late-night calls with Damien became increasingly frequent throughout the separation period. We started sharing personal details about our history and current happenings, including my new neighbor's interest in me.

This started a series of visits, including hugging and kissing, and an invitation for lunch on Valentine's Day. The night before Valentine's Day, I came home to find a bird cage with two parakeets, heart-shaped paper taped to the cage, and chocolate under the cage.

I had my hopes up again and believed Damien and I were best friends again. Lunch was nice! And that evening, when he came to pick up Jessie, we kissed and hugged for a while. I had plans to go out with Lisa to a Japanese restaurant. She encouraged me to try sushi for the first time, and I loved it. We went dancing afterward. Damien called me later that night to make sure I got home okay. We spoke on the telephone for a few hours. When he came by to pick Jessie up for a trip to Orlando for them to visit with his sister, he handed me a Valentine's Day card with a long note. The plan was for the two of us to work on some of our issues.

I also received a Valentine's Day card from the new neighbor.

But my heart remained with my husband, and it appeared restoration work was on the horizon. Our friendship was improving, and when he returned home late the following day after driving in the downpour rain to bring Jessie back home, it was decided he should just stay over since it was so late, and the weather was still horrible. And stay over he did, in my bed. The late-night hours were wonderfully spent. Things were looking up, or so I thought.

On the phone with Damien about a week later, I pronounced, "I love you." His response was dead silence. It kind of slipped out. The song from Foreigner came to mind, "Cold as Ice." Yeah, cold as ice—this man who just blessed me on Valentine's Day. I spoke into the phone again and inquired, "Are you cold again?"

He said he regretted our weekend, that it was a mistake and should not happen again.

Ouch.

Attempting to cope with this devastating news, I found myself at the store afterward to purchase a pack of cigarettes, even though I hate them. They stink. I smoked five anyway. I didn't think I would survive this.

Damien and Jessica had planned a day at Boomer's Park in Boca Raton. This place had it all: miniature golf, bumper boats, go-karts, laser tag, an arcade, and batting cages. I struggled with my need for companionship, so I asked if I could join them. All Damien did was remind me of our impending divorce. The whole day was painful, and I'd made a big mistake.

"Damien," I said, "I came to have fun—not to discuss our situation."

My desperate need to feel loved and wanted was overwhelming. I wanted to feel like I still had a family.

The conversation I had with my neighbor Sam came back to mind when he called me the day after giving me the Valentine's card. After sharing an update on how Damien and I were doing, I thanked him for the card and explained we would need to remain friends. We both were still technically married. I loved my husband and desired for our marriage to heal. He mentioned he was surprised and that he felt terrible. He asked himself out loud, "What am I doing to this girl?"

I wondered why my husband didn't care enough to ask himself this very question.

🪨 JEWELS 🪨

Dear precious one, the season of brokenness and despair from loss, death, abuse, sickness, or divorce feels like you're at the edge of hell. There are no quick fixes, easy solutions, or shortcuts to ease the pain. Reading about my season of brokenness is not pretty (and the journey continues throughout this book). Each of our paths differs in some regard or another, but we are all in process. No matter where you find yourself, do not be discouraged. When you are buried in the weeds, challenges come at you fast. Some may understand their value and worth much faster than others. When a marriage is breaking or dying, one may not even notice at first. Then, during the final stages of death, the dance of decisions is exhausting. Many of these decisions are destiny choices. We are human and will not always respond in the best manner.

What hurts are you still carrying? Who do you need to forgive? Forgiving does not excuse bad behavior. It frees you. My forgiveness work started with my husband, my family, in-laws, and finally myself. Dr. Kevin Leman informs us, "You need to forgive—not because your parents deserve forgiveness but because you deserve the freedom that comes from the act of forgiving."

A broken marriage can experience healing and restoration. Odds increase for this healing when both hearts remain focused on God, find support and counseling, and keep distractions away. Commitment to the marriage of both partners is critical, with no third party in the mix (this could be a person or an addiction). God had a plan for my healing journey, involving many different people, places, and organizations. I had to walk through my circumstances, and I did the best I could at that time. You can, too, one day at a time.

"When fear is running your life, you will not be true to yourself. It takes vigilance and an honest commitment to move you from the life you have to the life you want. But being true to yourself is the key that will get you there," said Rhonda Britten.

It may not be clear what is happening or what your future may hold. Be encouraged by these scriptures:

"The Lord opens the eyes of the blind. The Lord raises up those who are brought down. The Lord loves those who are right and good" (Psalm 146:8 NLV).

"You have shown me many troubles of all kinds. But you will make me strong again. And you will bring me up again from deep in the earth" (Psalm 71:20 NLV).

"The Lord is my strength and my safe cover. My heart trusts in Him, and I am helped. So, my heart is full of joy. I will thank Him with my song" (Psalm 28:7 NLV).

"For He has not turned away from the suffering of the one in pain or trouble. He has not hidden His face from him. But He has heard his cry for help" (Psalm 22: 24 NLV).

My healing came through the various ups and downs and the back and forth of circumstances, much like the ebb and flow of ocean waves. With each wave, the jewels are sifted out from the junk until, at last, we clearly see them rising to the surface. Your rescue was only the beginning. Walking through the days afterward is where you find your way to higher ground.

Go easy on yourself and everyone around you. It will be imperative to reach out for help. Start with a phone call to a friend or an agency within your community. Find a good, Jesus-loving, faith-based, Biblical church family to plug into. Protect your heart. Get to know your Abba Father. He loves you best, and He has the power to help. A lot is happening that is beyond your control and understanding. The junk can be overwhelming to sort through and discard.

You are loved! "For God so loved the world that He gave his only Son. Whoever puts his trust in God's Son will not be lost but will have life that lasts forever" (John 3:16 NLV). "The Lord opens the eyes of the blind. The Lord raises up those who are brought down. The Lord loves those who are right and good" (Psalm 146:8 NLV). Just like God heard and saw me while on the floor of my closet, set up His rescue, and held my hand through all that came afterward, He has you, too, my friend. Trust in Him. Your edge of Hell will not last forever. This is your one-of-a-kind moment to gain clarity in your conditions. And never give up!

Never give in! Never give in! Never, never, never, never—in nothing great and small—large and petty—never give in except to conviction of honor and good sense.

—WINSTON CHURCHILL

CHAPTER 4

Clarity in Conditions

"The more you go with the flow of life and surrender the outcome to God, and the less you seek constant clarity, the more you will find that fabulous things start to show up in your life."

—MANDY HALE,
The Single Woman: Life, Love, and a Dash of Sass

Damien had come over to the apartment after I returned home from a memorial service. Both of us cried, and he said he did not want our marriage to end in a divorce, but he did not wish to talk to anyone or work on anything. He would always be the way he is. He brought champagne and toasted to peace, apologizing for being mean and angry with me.

He stayed the night. We were going to work on our friendship, but I didn't set proper boundaries. I shouldn't have slept with him, but I did, and the uncertainty messed with me. He should not have had the privileges of a husband if he was not acting like a husband, but that was a lesson learned in hindsight.

There were plans for a date night the following night, but something in me felt different.

I knew this was not what God wanted for me.

"God, I'm confused. I want to do what's right. My heart has changed. I have changed. I am happy now, more than ever, but I also miss

Damien. I don't miss how it was, our lifestyle, being disappointed and ignored. I've had enough of that. I want to be with people who want to be with me."

The phone rang, and it was Delilah (not her real name, of course). She was a woman my husband had met on his mission trip before we officially separated. When they'd returned, I thought she and Damien had something going on from their time in Haiti. Wouldn't you think something was fishy if you entered the church and a woman skipped down the aisle toward you shouting your husband's name, "Damien, Damien, Damien!"?

What was going on? I suffered in silence, wondering for days after they returned until a note came that confirmed my thinking there may be more to worry about, and that gave me the courage to confront the two of them. It was from Delilah, and it read,

"Afterthoughts of Haiti,

Dear Damien, the blessings, joys, tears, and mostly love will be forever in our hearts! I can only look forward to returning to continue the good work! I also want to thank you … for always being there! You were such a great help not only to me but to everyone! I pray God blesses you over and abundantly with more than your heart can handle! You are special.

Love in Christ always,

Delilah."

What married woman writes a personal note like this to a married man? Seriously?!! I had to say something. When I confronted them, they both assured me nothing was going on. I felt foolish for thinking there was. Maybe I was extra sensitive in this area because it almost happened to me—an affair—with someone who was my "friend," the man who worked at the boys' home I volunteered at and had paid me special attention.

I sent her flowers to apologize. She seemed to truly care that Damien and I were working things out, and I needed all the friends I could get. My suspicions were correct, though. I wasn't foolish.

This was another roller coaster ride of sorts. I struggled with my thoughts and need for companionship as my husband and I drifted further apart and began the process of separation and divorce. My relationship with Sam, the neighbor, was not helping my current emotional state. The temptation to be with him was overpowering. The need to be loved, cared for, and liked by someone was too great for me to handle. He continued to pursue me, especially when his mother shared details from my conversation with her on the status of my broken marriage and Damien's current attitude toward me.

I went to church Wednesday night, needing answers from God. During the altar call, while I was on my knees praying and being prayed for, my pastor mentioned he sensed something had happened to me even before I got married. I was feeling mangled and muddled.

"I don't know," I said, "Damien was my first and only."

He asked about my family.

I cried out, "What family?"

He had his answer. "Is, or was, your father an alcoholic?" my pastor asked.

"Yes," I replied.

My pastor explained, "You never knew intimacy. You tried to fill that void with Damien by being with him, by having sex."

I had my head down in shame, and he made me look at him. He said, "Georgette, you do not need a man to feel loved or valued."

The pastor dismissed the church service and asked me and other church members to stay and pray with me.

Margaret noticed my bare finger and asked where my wedding ring was. "Why did you take it off?" she asked.

I whimpered, "If he doesn't want me …."

The pastor and church members immediately started praying for me and rebuked and bound doublemindedness. Miss Margaret was the first to pray out loud, and she told me to put my band back on and to make sure the relationship with my neighbor was over. My pastor had seven women agree to call me each night for twenty-eight days for accountability. I was warned: once clean, it will be seven times worse if they come back.

Though it wasn't easy, I gave my will to God. I got home around 10:00 p.m. and felt utterly free for the first time in a long time. I walked on the treadmill, listened to my Christian music video, worshipped God, and prayed in the Spirit.

Sam, the neighbor downstairs, continued to interact with me. He asked me if I would *be* with him, but I was petrified that I would move away from God. I did not want to mess up; I was in a dangerous place. I told Sam we would be friends, a decision I'm immensely grateful to have made. My struggle with Sam finally ended.

The covering over my eyes finally came off, and I saw how selfish he was. I admit to seeing some of this in him, but it all came together for me one night.

God gave me such strength and answered my prayers to change my will to be His, and I was able to say NO. I got very angry over the whole situation. Suddenly, things were clear as day. I was mad at Sam for his selfishness. I was mad at myself for allowing my insecurities to take over. I was mad at Damien for not caring about trying to work things out between us.

When it was clear that I would not sleep with Sam, he left. At this point, his motives were obvious. I grabbed my bike and headed down the stairs. After racing around our complex a few times, I sat on one of the curbs, cried, and talked with God. I was still so angry.

When Delilah called to talk, déjà vu hit me hard. The hope once residing in my heart bottomed out, but I tried to hold on to it. I didn't know about her relationship with Damien yet, and I gave her the updates. One of the experiences I shared with her in detail was the night Jessie and I went up to the altar for prayer. Jessica was getting prayed for, and I glanced around. There was Jamie Parsons, the guest speaker, down on his knees, praying. I was humbled and touched. It dramatically affected me.

God had provided clarity in the type of man I could pray for. In my heart of hearts, I knew this was the kind of man I desired above all: a man who loved God with all his heart. Serving God with a man who loves God as I do would be a true gift. Would that be Damien? Would God do a work in his heart? I had no idea, but now I knew what the possibility was for me in the future.

* * *

On one particular night during our separation, I became fed up with the back-and-forth with Damien. I called him with two questions: One, does he want to start over? Yes or no? Two, will he commit to just one day a week for us to go out for a date night and keep Sundays as a family day? Oh, and he would need to get some counseling. He could not commit.

Damien ended up coming over that evening after 10:00 p.m. to talk. I was not afraid to be alone for the first time in ten months. I liked my routine and freedom and could not picture him moving back in and fitting into my new life. But I was torn. I still loved Damien so much that it hurt. I did not want a divorce. I explained to him that marriage is a partnership, and I would not be able to hold it alone anymore.

* * *

Boundaries invite self-respect and guard against resentment. The bravest and boldest action we can take for ourselves is to learn how to set boundaries and hold ourselves accountable to them.

I gave my husband access to me no matter how he treated me, even when he was not committed to the relationship. This was the pattern before he officially moved out. He was never home, coming and going wherever and whenever without me knowing. He acted like he had no responsibilities as a husband. I showed my desperation every time he called and said "yes" to his requests, no matter what time. Every time he walked out the door again, not knowing the future or when he would return home, it sliced my heart even more.

Eventually, I came to learn that having healthy boundaries in place would make me more respected in the long run and send a clear message. I learned how to respect myself, and I had the potential to earn the respect of others, including my partner. If I had no idea how my partner chose to live or who he may decide to be with, allowing him access to me jeopardized my mental and physical health.

Abstinence would have been the healthier option. Time apart could have brought greater clarity to my situation. Oh, the gems hindsight and hard-earned wisdom bring. In the moment, I did the best I could do.

I realized later that while I could keep my heart open toward my spouse, allowing hope for reconciliation, I did not have to sleep with him. Yes to friendship and our being kind toward each other. But a big N-O to allowing him full access to all parts of me when he deliberately made it clear he was no longer committed.

This truth came slowly, ever so slowly, to me. The wound of abandonment and rejection was rooted deep within me from my childhood and previous generations. I did not realize my self-worth, until, after too many times of being used and made to feel worthless, I learned the root cause sometime later. God revealed truth in this area by slowly pulling back the layers of history and time. He reminded me of when we first got married and returned from our honeymoon. Damien had a planned hunting trip in Vermont with his brother and their friend. Yes, the same brother who took him to a strip club for his bachelor party. I can't remember how soon after he left; it may have been the first night. I freaked out and didn't even understand what it was I had experienced then. I over-drank and got sick and remembered calling my mom. I think I may have gone home. The whole time my husband was away was a horrible time, and I struggled to be alone. Then God reminded me about my trip to Poland with my mom, aunt, and grandmother. My grandmother had not seen her sister since World War II, and the trip was a huge occasion for them to reunite and for all of us to meet our Polish relatives. We stayed with my grandmother's sister, my great aunt. The whole household spoke Polish. Sometime during our stay, my mother and aunt were invited to go hiking in the mountains, which involved a ten-day excursion. They left the next morning without telling me. I woke up to find her gone. For many years, I believed I was 8 ½ years old. But only very recently, after finding my actual passport from the trip, did I realize I was only 6 ½ years old. No one meant any harm, but I was affected deeply and came to understand this as my root for fear of abandonment and explained why I held on to relationships at all costs, even to my own detriment. This included fear of loss of love. I also came to know about some of the generational abandonments experienced by my mom, dad, and their parents. My own grandmother and mother were abandoned by their fathers and mothers, including emotional abandonment. My father experienced emotional abandonment as well. During my master's degree studies, I learned about significant attachment theory and how this affected all my relationships and further explained why being alone or left was something I worked so hard to avoid.

Saying no to what was an obvious circumstance to me now was a new beginning. And, again, a start that did not happen soon enough. Heck, I had been the girl who still wanted to be friends with a girl after she threw me in the pricker bushes (true story from my grammar school days). I seemed to be okay with accepting crumbs—until I wasn't.

* * *

Damien asked for the attorney's number to start the filing process. I told him again I did not want a divorce. He said, "Fine. We will just do all the paperwork and financial statements." I had a hard time accepting that our marriage could end after all these years.

If Damien wanted to stay, he would have gotten therapy. In over a year, Damien was still detached, hard-hearted, and angry toward me. He focused on my negative qualities and mess-ups and seemed to take great pleasure in judging me. He had no desire to hold on to our marriage for any of the worthy reasons, like Jessica, our beautiful, precious daughter.

This was no way to live.

The paperwork was finally completed and needed Damien's signature. He didn't file the papers and, for a time, said he could not find them. I sought counsel from my church leaders, and one of my pastors counseled that I was released by God. My husband had abandoned me and Jessica. He had no intention of ever coming back home, nor did he desire to seek counseling or provide financial support. I would have to file the papers with the court. Once the papers were "found," I did just that. Divorce papers were served, and mediation was set up.

During this season of hardship and growth, I experienced a revelation, a new understanding of what it felt like to be heard. I was chatting with the new attractive neighbor (as we girls called him) while he was washing his truck, and we were having a noble conversation about our relationships. Greg, another neighbor, came over and chatted with us for a bit. Then, both the guys started discussing something else. When I interjected to ask them a question, the new, attractive neighbor stopped talking to Greg for a minute, answered my question, and continued. I was shocked!

The whole interaction had a profound effect on me. I did not expect people to hear me, much less listen. It was a nice feeling. A feeling I was not familiar with. I always felt ignored by Damien—like a shadow. I had to talk louder to be heard or repeat myself a thousand times to be heard or noticed.

* * *

I was about to turn thirty years old, and Jessica was seven. Life was busy, but I spent sleepless nights crying out to God about the divorce settlement. *God, please make it something I can live with and can handle, especially in my current living and bill conditions.* I was in over my head. I couldn't pay all the bills and desperately needed money. I got a job waiting tables at Chili's.

Damien wanted nothing to do with me. He was considering filing for bankruptcy. My brain was bombarded with many thoughts. *If he goes bankrupt, what's keeping him here in Florida?* He planned to take Jessica to Connecticut next weekend for about ten days. I did not trust him.

I went home, collapsed on my bed, and wept. I was barely able to pray.

Oh, God. I am exhausted. This pain is unbearable. Why am I fighting so hard for this relationship? Why am I holding on to someone who has made it repeatedly clear with his words and actions that I don't matter to him? And why to this same man, a man who, through-out our years of marriage, showed by his actions I was not a valued partner? Maybe I am afraid this makes me a horrible Christian, or maybe not even a Christian. Maybe I am holding on out of fear of the unknown? Or is it because I am fighting not to be abandoned or rejected at all costs? I love him but do not love how he has treated me. I do not love how our relationship has been so dysfunctional. You have tried showing me my worth and how a healthy relationship takes two. It is a mutual partnership. This will not work if neither party is accountable for their respective parts. I work hard to never fail, and divorcing would feel like a failure. This inner conflict needs a resolution. Please help me. Please have mercy on me. Please send some miracles this way.

 **JEWELS**

Pain has a purpose. Did your eyes just roll? Seriously, pain does have a purpose. It does. There's nothing quite like some good-ole pain to get our attention. Pain makes us aware of unsafe or unhealthy choices and circumstances. Pain lets us know something is wrong. Truthfully, pain is involved in most miraculous breakthroughs, growth, and new beginnings. Conquering a new land or territory or gaining new ground usually brings some type of pain. But this truth is life-changing, for the better, when we embrace its healing work and allow it to guide our notions. Truth revealed brings pain.

For me, it was through repeated heart and emotional pain that I gained clarity. I seem to have a higher threshold for it than some. But I finally saw the light, and when it was time, this new truth about myself and my newfound self-worth helped me make changes. Vickie L. Milazzo instructs us, "To conceive any vision, you must first get quiet. Remove the clutter and turn down the volume. Consciously eliminate pervasive noise. Silence arouses imagination." You can start small by incorporating three easy steps Vickie recommends:

1. Clear your space.

2. Unclutter your mind.

3. Put off procrastination.

Oprah said, "There is a sacred calling on each of our lives. Whether you know it or not, it is your job to find out what that calling is and get about the business of doing it." Become a detective on your own self and research what makes you tick. Who are you? Learning about my birth order personality details was eye-opening, and even better was understanding my family members' birth order. I understood many of our family dynamics much better. Dr. Leman's book *Have a New You by Friday* explains birth order traits, but you can also Google it. Your future is up to you. He declares, "The past has already influenced your present, but how much it influences your future is up to you." and "Successful people usually have as many bad memories as "regular" people do. The difference is that successful people use their bad memories as motivation to create good memories."

We gain strength from our many mistakes by paying attention to what the mistakes tell us. Are we where we want to be in life? Who are we? Are my behaviors, or the behaviors of others, in alignment with the truth? If someone says they love or care for us, are they consistently showing it? Words matter, but actions matter more.

Bold and beautiful boundaries protect us and keep our respect intact. But boundaries can only be placed when one understands when and where they belong and why they belong there. You may not see your situation clearly right away. It sure took me a while to understand the boundaries concept for myself, others, and my husband.

Baby steps are okay. "If you do not have wisdom, ask God for it. He is always ready to give it to you and will never say you are wrong for asking"

(James 1:5 NLV). I talked to and asked God about everything. You can, too. He is there for you. Answers come in various ways at the perfect time.

At the beginning of our pre-separation and separation period, I needed to be held by my husband. This made me feel loved. Because he was still my husband, I thought it was okay. But, later, it became clear he was amid his own conflict of guilt and conviction. He would express love, then treat me as less than. Finally, when his commitment failed, and his decision not to pursue help or agree to some changes was clear, it was time for those beautiful, bold boundaries. I even had to back away from other family members whose focus seemed to be on my faults and who could not provide support. You may have to do this as well. This is painful, but it's okay. Taking a step back does not mean the relationship is over. You are gaining perspective.

It will be worthwhile to research and study attachment theory. Doing so will provide you with solid information to understand how early relationships can shape your emotional and social development throughout your life. You will glean knowledge to help you understand how you form and maintain relationships and how you respond to stress. There is importance to your childhood bond with your parents, and if there was disruption or loss of this bond, how it affected you emotionally and psychologically follows you into adulthood and has an impact on future relationships. Several generations of family members and I did not have secure bonds with our parents, which explained much of my family dynamics. And it will explain much for you as well. Do not worry if you do not have secure attachments with your parents or others. God can heal even this. He will help you develop a secure attachment with Him and, from there, heal you from the past. Deliverance is a delightful endeavor, as it is a game-changer for future relationship choices. More on this in the pages to come!

Participating in various self-help groups can be life-changing. Gaining other perspectives may be what is needed. "I will show you and teach you in the way you should go. I will tell you what to do with My eye upon you" (Psalms 32:8 NLV). God shows us what to do through other people, books, podcasts, and other creative ways. Clarity comes through our conditions and the surrendering of these conditions—even through our pain. Fingerprints of faith graciously reveal themselves in due time. Beautiful friend, "Every day brings a chance for you to draw in a breath, kick off your shoes, and dance" (Oprah Winfrey). My daughter and I would dance together often, and I danced solo many nights. What a fun, empowering activity! Go ahead, play your favorite tunes, and let loose!

> *When my spirit grows faint within me, it is*
> *you who watch over my way.*
>
> **—PSALM 142:3 (NIV)**

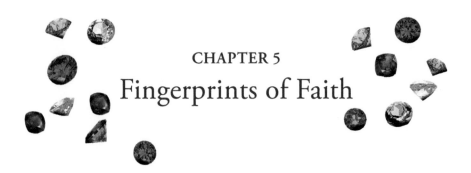

CHAPTER 5

Fingerprints of Faith

*"Don't miss God's fingerprints all over the events, lining up
people and circumstances in perfect timing to preserve
His people and advance His agenda."*

—JAMES MACDONALD

The necklace I wore became a meaningful message from God. It was a gold heart with footprints imprinted on it, symbolizing the "Footprints in the Sand" poem (Mary Stevenson, 1939). God's fingerprints showed up in every part of my life, and this message of hope became my new reality. God does carry me, and God does lift my burdens.

God's rescue mission of love was carried out with perfect precision as layers of His care unfolded for my daughter and me. Upon our arrival in Florida, we were graciously and miraculously placed within the Pinewood Pointe Apartments community. God immediately stabilized our situation and divinely set plans for our new home and community in motion. He knew what I did not at the time: the outcome of my marriage. Placement in this community would prove to be momentous.

The word "pinewood" was first used in 1601 and is defined as the wood of a pine tree or the wood or growth of pines (Merriam-Webster). Pines (firs) inhabited the "good lands" of Lebanon, "The glory of Lebanon shall come to you, The cypress, the pine, and the box tree together, To beautify the place of My sanctuary; And I will make the place of My feet glorious" (Isiah 60:13 NKJV).

From spiritualbotany.com, I learned that "pines (Pinus spp.) have permeated into the folklore of many cultures, being associated with immortality, steadiness, and resilience possibly due to their successful adaptation to diverse and often harsh environments, as well as their longevity in nature." The same source explains that the first Christmas, or Nativity, tree was likely a pine tree meant to symbolize life.

God was strategic in placing our broken family at Pinewood Pointe Apartments. The richness of the relationships we made during our years living there was priceless. Every resident in our building, whether short-term or long-term, added value and meaning to our lives and brought life-changing insights and lessons.

God placed me on a perch to observe others as they lived their daily lives. These ongoing observations instilled in my heart many life truths. My perch on the corner of our building made it possible for me to engage with our neighbors as they came or went. We got to know each other through simple greetings in passing. These moments brought a smile and a hope-filled nudge toward living. The community I found in our new home kept loneliness at bay.

Tom and Julia, a precious couple and fast friends, looked out for Jessica and me. They became trusted guides and shining lights to emulate as I proceeded as a single mom, growing in my own life. Both were people of faith who loved God and people, and their actions proved it. They sowed goodness, and I got a front-row seat as they reaped the harvest of what they planted. We often sat together and shared meaningful conversations. I recall Tom once sharing with me that he and Julia had never once spent a night apart in all the years they were married. Their love for each other was visible, and my heart warmed every time I saw them walk over to the pool, hand in hand. I loved gleaning wisdom from these two love birds.

Kacey and Lara also became beautiful friends of ours, and I bore witness to the life changes and growth in our respective families. Lara and I would have many conversations together through the years about life and my hopes of finding my future mate.

* * *

I will never forget the words my spiritual mentor, Joyce, spoke to me during our women's Bible study meeting. God prompted me to take notice of the date, July 31, 1997. Joyce shared that I was like a bouquet of flowers blooming. This affirmation was fulfilled over time. God was bringing me to life, and His touches have never stopped. Let go and let God because He carries us in ways we could never fathom.

A "gut instinct" helped me find a top job with better hours and circumstances. It was time to leave the nonprofit I worked for. To provide for my daughter and myself, I needed a forty-hour job with benefits, so I decided to return to the insurance industry and submitted applications to a few agencies.

I was offered a position and accepted, but instead of the two-week notice I wished to provide my current employer, they needed me in a week. After giving one week's notice, I received a phone call on my last day of work that they had given the job to another candidate. Since our qualifications were similar, their only explanation for the change was a "gut instinct."

Despite the fear of not knowing what would come next, I went home that day in peace. I returned a call to another insurance agency, one that had previously desired to interview me as well and was offered the position. This employer was in property and casualty insurance, which I had experience with, whereas the other was in life and health. The pay was higher; parking was provided; the commute was shorter, and the benefits were better. God placed me in the perfect place.

The other agency called me a few weeks afterward because they wished to hire me again. The person they'd hired had left. I couldn't help but think about how God knows what He is doing. He will *always* work out situations and events for our good and His glory.

God carried me and provided for me in so many ways through various people and experiences.

One day, a client of the insurance agency I worked for as a customer service representative came in to say that God had placed me on his heart and that everything would work out. He came in just to share that encouragement.

I experienced a coincidental meeting at the beach, where Jessie and I found ourselves almost every weekend. Being in nature and soaking in sunshine's vitamin C along the shore was both healing and inexpensive. I had decided to treat Jessie to a hot dog and had the extra cash on me, which was not normal for us. We headed over to the Sand Dune Café, and as we made our way to the dock stairs, I noticed, out of the corner of my eye, a guy leaning on the rails, staring right at me.

I looked up and said, "Hi, how's it going?"

After we ordered, we stepped aside to let the next person place their order and waited for our food. Something felt odd. There was that guy again, but he was now in front of me. I stared back, and then it hit me: I knew him.

"Ken?"

"Georgette?! Georgette!"

He even remembered my long Polish last name. I knew him from high school; he was a senior when I was a freshman, and I'd had a crush on him all year—along with almost every other girl. After he graduated, I didn't see him again until years later when I joined a new gym, and he was assigned as my personal trainer. And here he was now in Florida! It was a divine appointment.

Ken was glad to see me, and I, him. We exchanged phone numbers and spent the rest of the day together. He shared with me that his wife had left him for another man two months prior. This chance meeting brought a bright spot into my life, and God used me to encourage him, which ultimately brought me more joy.

But my heart desired romance, and falling into old patterns would be too easy. I had slowly come to realize the importance of saying no. While there was no pressure from Ken, for the first time, thinking about saying no to a man wasn't bad. I needed to be pursued, not the pursuer—this was hard to grasp, and I learned this through years of doing it wrong.

I remember when I heard about the opera *La Boehme*. I had always wanted to experience opera, especially after seeing the movie *Pretty Woman*, so when the show was coming to our area, I planned to get tickets.

As I punched in the code at the ATM to get cash for the tickets, I felt a bit guilty. That money would be needed to pay upcoming bills.

Jessie and I went to the window to buy our tickets. While I was asking about the seating arrangements, a lady approached the other window and said, "Here, what should I do with these? I have two tickets I don't need."

The ladies behind the windows pointed at me and said, "Give them to her!" Praise God! When He sets out to give us a special gift just because He loves us, He goes all out! Not only did we go to the opera at no cost, but we also got front-row seats. It was a beautiful show—the story, the music, everything was spectacular. Jessie loved all the beautiful costumes and enjoyed the songs. I loved listening to the gorgeous language. God blessed both of us, and we got to experience our very first opera together!

My new boss had encouraged me to take classes to obtain a property and casualty insurance license so that I could become an insurance agent/producer and sell policies. This would allow me to earn commissions on policies I sold. The only problem—the same problem as always—was that I had no extra money to pay the required application fee. I prayed about it and asked God for help.

While Jessica was playing one day, she decided she needed my Living Bible that was in the bookcase. She was going through the pages and out fell a white envelope. Inside the envelope was $100! At some point, I had placed money in my Bible to save for the future. I had forgotten all about it, but God never forgot. That money would cover the application fee. It was His plan all along for such a time as this. I received an extra bonus through the insurance class when God provided a whole new group of friends.

JEWELS

God carries and provides for you. You may not see His hands at first, but as you move through your crisis and challenging situations, take time daily to sit with God in prayer and meditation. He will reveal the various fingerprints of faith to you.

Remember how "pinewood" came to have much significance for me? God orchestrated details to place my daughter and me in a community named "Pinewood Pointe." He wished to provide a physical community with symbolic spiritual meaning attached so I would feel secure. I would experience steadiness and resilience of my own as my walk with the Lord progressed.

My dear one, God wants you to know how precious you are to Him. Take time to reflect and stay attuned to His working in you and your circumstances. Your fingerprints of faith will be unique to you and for you.

God exhibited his love through my neighbors, job placement, divine appointments, serendipitous front-row opera seats, perfectly timed words of encouragement, much-needed funds, and miraculous protection.

God has you in His hands, under His care. Your jewels will appear in the junk if you look for them. Thank God for them. Your fingerprints of faith will emerge, bolstering your faith and instilling hope. Your Junk to Jewels story will be one meant to encourage you and others. In your faith journey, moments of despair come face to face with miracles.

You do not need to know precisely what is happening or exactly where it is all going. What you need is to recognize the possibilities and challenges offered by the present moment and to embrace them with courage, faith, and hope.

—THOMAS MERTON

CHAPTER 6
Dental Despair

"I called on the Lord in distress; the Lord answered me
and set me in a broad place. The Lord is on my side;
I will not fear. What can man do to me?"

—PSALM 118:5-6 KJV

Jessica needed work done on her teeth. There was no more avoiding it, and I was beside myself. I was hardly managing to pay the rent or any other bills, and there was never extra money. I felt such guilt and sorrow for not having what we needed. Now, her teeth needed to be taken care of, and we didn't have insurance.

We were amid the living death that is divorce. Well, separation, limbo land, technically. There was no relief—only uncertainty.

The school was offering free dental clinic spots to those who needed financial assistance, and I signed her right up.

As I was reading through the note they sent back with her, I asked her how it went.

"They told me to tell my mommy to call my dentist."

I made it a point to finish reading through the paperwork from the dental clinic. Sure enough, per their notes, she needed a follow-up with her dentist soon and had a cavity that needed to be filled. Apparently, this was not included in the free dental evaluation.

Jessica, sweet and always aware of the feelings of others, was a favorite of all her teachers. She looked just like me with her brown hair and eyes. Her kindergarten picture was identical to mine. She loved to read and play with her baby dolls. She and I loved going to the beach and swimming in the apartment's pool together.

I put off scheduling an appointment for as long as I could, but when Jessica came home from school telling me her mouth was hurting, I began to search for a dentist. Every dentist I called said I would need to pay for services the day of the appointment.

No appointment was made.

Then Jessica woke up in the middle of the night crying. I applied some gel to ease the pain. The next day, I received a call from the school nurse. I explained the situation and gave her permission to give Jessica some liquid Tylenol.

I found the courage to pick up the telephone and call the dental office that had hosted the dental clinic. I did this in faith, hoping they would allow me to make payments until it was paid off. An appointment was scheduled. I was sick with worry. We needed a miracle.

When that day came, I still did not have the money for her appointment. I called to reschedule for the following week and explained my situation more fully to them. After realizing my financial situation and learning that my daughter had been in discomfort and, more recently, pain, they agreed to let me make three payments. I was still apprehensive. How was I even going to pay the first one? I had prayed specifically for a miracle. I asked God for the money needed. Either a check would come in, or there would be someone I could borrow money from.

I almost canceled the new appointment to allow more time to pass in the hopes that some extra money would miraculously come to me. It didn't, but I couldn't cancel the appointment again. Jessica was now in too much discomfort. We were going to the dentist office anyway, believing in my heart that God would take care of Jessica.

Jessie was crying in her sleep again. The alarm went off much too early, and I didn't want to wake up. I had been up for most of the night with Damien on the phone, arguing and crying.

I was on a roller coaster ride. One minute, I was feeling OK and hopeful, but the next, I felt devastated and empty. I had moments of willing my heart to stop beating, but also had moments of clarity. I could not—would not—leave my daughter. I would not abandon her. It was shocking how life could go on amid the slow death of a marriage. Everything was on my shoulders now. Every decision, problem, and bill to be paid was on me.

While the coffee was brewing, I headed into Jessie's room to wake her up. "Good morning, Jessie." I leaned over to give her a kiss on her soft cheek. "Time to get up, honey. Today's your dentist appointment. Rise and shine."

She put her arms around my head and said, "OK."

"You are such a cute little girl. Mommy loves you." She loved it when I kissed her all over, and I loved hearing her giggles. She was smiling. I hugged her tightly and then headed toward her door.

"Mommy is going to shower while you get dressed. We have to hurry, or we'll be late. After breakfast, brush your teeth well."

When I got dressed, Jessie was already waiting at the door, smiling at me with toothpaste on the side of her mouth. She was utterly adorable. I grabbed the kitchen towel and wiped her mouth.

"You beat me to the door today. I'm impressed!"

"Are you happy, Mommy?"

"My heart's always happy because I get to be your mommy!" My heart melted and then broke again. She didn't deserve the pains of a broken home—broken because her parents were unable to work things out. How was that fair? There was no time for thinking about this right now. Mornings were usually a hard push to get where we both needed to be, and today was no exception.

Thank goodness the dentist's office was not even five minutes up the road.

We got in the car, put our seatbelts on, and turned on Christian FM radio. One of our favorite songs by Audio Adrenaline was playing, and we both started singing.

The appointment was for 8:00 a.m. My watch showed 8:02 a.m. as we walked into the office. I was shaking as I signed us in, and we waited. My stomach hurt. I knew I wouldn't have enough money to pay the whole first payment, and I dreaded the soon-to-be conversation. My prayers were nonstop.

> *God, I know you'll help us somehow. You know I had to do it this way. You know I always follow the rules and would never try to take advantage of anyone. But this is different; Jessie needs help. God, you're all we have. Please help her. Have mercy on me, please.*

They had some children's toys out, which quickly got Jessie's attention. I hoped my smile was big enough for Jessie to believe it.

"Jessica?"

"That's us. Come on, Jessica."

The woman was pleasant and had a nice smile. She helped Jessica into the big chair.

"I like your bracelet. It's gorgeous!"

This brought a chuckle and a big smile to the dental hygienist. "Why thank you, Miss Jessica! I found it while on vacation in Mexico last year." As she got her equipment ready, she looked over at me.

"Mom looks like she's more nervous than you are, Jessica."

I smiled, and Jessica laughed. "Mommy's nervous for me."

"It's going to be OK, Mom. We'll just be cleaning her teeth and taking some X-rays today."

"Sound great," I replied as I sat down on the chair in the corner facing them both. I was super proud of my daughter. She was so brave. The woman was gentle and extremely patient. I tried to keep my smile on.

"Mom, you have a beautiful little girl who is being so good."

"Thank you. She is a good girl."

"Jessica, are you brushing your teeth every day?"

Jessica nodded.

"Outstanding! It's very important to brush daily and to take your time when you brush. OK, we are finished. I will meet you both out in the front office."

"Thank you very much."

"Jessica was so good; I think she deserves more than one lollipop. What do you think, Mom?"

"Yes, I agree."

"I will bring out your lollipops shortly, OK, Jessica?"

Jessica smiled and hurried out of the chair. At the doorway, she turned around and ran back to hug the woman. I saw that it caught her off guard but was well received. I got up and quickly followed Jessica into the waiting room.

We did not wait long. The dental assistant came out to meet us, and Jessica rushed over to her.

"Here you go, sweetheart. Take your pick. Thank you for being such a good patient today."

"Thank you," she replied, selecting three different colors.

"You are very welcome. What a polite young lady you are. Mom, would it be alright if I followed you outside to speak with you for a moment?"

"Sure, but I have to take care of some things with the receptionist first."

"Oh, no need. You are all set right now. We can head out to your car."

She opened the door for us, and we all walked outside and headed over to where my car was parked right outside the entrance.

After helping Jessie in, I carefully shut the door and faced the dental assistant. She must think I am a horrible mother, as her eyes were full of unshed tears.

"I saw your little girl laying in the chair, a beautiful, sweet, innocent little girl. She was an angel, a precious, beautiful angel. I looked over at you, her mom. A mom who is on her own trying to take care of her daughter the best she can. The condition of Jessica's teeth requires immediate dental care that can no longer be put off."

Something inside me was going to break open as I looked into this woman's eyes, a stranger to me. She was crying.

"I want to help you. I hope you will let me. My husband and I are very blessed. We never got to have children of our own. Will you let me help you?"

My eyes watered up as goosebumps went up and down my arms. If this were any other time or situation, I would say no. I knew to accept.

"Good. Just call our office later today, and schedule your next appointment. Your daughter will have to come for three separate appointments."

"Okay. Thank you." I started to say more but couldn't speak. I was overwhelmed. I could feel the tears rolling down my cheeks.

She hugged me, and I hugged her back. After she waved to Jessie, she went back inside.

I took Jessie to school, trying not to cry in front of her.

"Mommy, are you OK?"

I nodded. "Yes, sweetie. Mommy is OK. Do you know how much I love you?"

"Yes, you love me this much." Her arms went as wide as they could go.

I squeezed her hand. "Yes, I love you this much." I extended my longer arms as far as I could extend them. I headed to work after dropping her off. The weeping would have to wait.

Later that afternoon, I called the office and made her appointments. I was not sure how she was going to help us, but I knew enough now not to worry. I sensed God had it all under control. I was completely taken by surprise. God covered the shame I was feeling with sweetness from a kind stranger.

When we arrived Monday morning for Jessica's appointment, the dental assistant greeted me in the waiting room and handed me an envelope. I hugged her hard as I thanked her profusely. Instead of being judged, I was seen with grace and given mercy. Instead of criticism, I was given help.

She held out her hand as she said, "Jessica, are you ready?"

I did not open the envelope right then. When it was time to pay for the appointment and schedule the next one, I opened the envelope and took out the cash. There was $600.00, so our bill was paid in full.

A mercy miracle arrived in full through the heart of another.

JEWELS

God shows up. He responds to the cries of our hearts. He is our help in the midst of crisis. God showing up like He did in response to my daughter's dental needs made me feel seen and loved. I was encouraged and remembered this ultimate care many times in the years to come. This miracle story was selected as a 2018 Writer's Digest Writing Competition Award Winner.

You are not alone, even if it may feel that way at times. I encourage you to read your Bible. Not only does God speak to each of us personally through His Words, but one gains confidence from the many promises written and receives hope for one's own challenges because the stories where God helps His people over and over again seep through our hearts and minds. We can face our tomorrows with greater faith.

> *Believe in miracles. I have seen so many of them come when every other indication would say that hope was lost. Hope is never lost.*
>
> **—JEFFREY R. HOLLAND**

CHAPTER 7

Bitter or Better

"You either get bitter, or you get better. It's that simple. You either take what has been dealt to you and allow it to make you a better person, or you allow it to tear you down. The choice does not belong to fate; it belongs to you."

—JOSH SHIPP

In my time alone with God, I found healing, hope, forgiveness, understanding, and deliverance through prayer and meditation. In my journal pages, I found God, the real God of love and compassion. He meets us where we are—despite our junk.

"Mindfulness provides a simple but powerful route for getting ourselves unstuck, back into touch with our own wisdom and vitality. It is a way to take charge of the direction and quality of our own lives, including our relationships within the family, our relationship to work and to the larger world and planet, and most fundamentally, our relationship with ourself as a person," said by Jon Kabat-Zinn in *Wherever You Go, There You Are: Mindfulness Meditation in Everyday Life*. He goes on to say, "When we commit ourselves to paying attention in an open way, without falling prey to our own likes and dislikes, opinions and prejudices, projections and expectations, new possibilities open up, and we have a chance to free ourselves from the straitjacket of unconsciousness."

Journaling has been an impactful tool for me since I was a young girl. I have heart-to-heart conversations with God and write my pains, questions, and needs in my journals. I also write out my praises to God and all I am grateful for. I added praying for others to my daily writing time with God.

Spending time alone with God opened the door for me to hear from Him directly. As I wrote, God would impart revelations, and I gained new understanding, discernment, and perspective, helping to set me free.

I recall how, in one week, I received two revelations from God. One night, as I listened to my music through my headphones, I paid close attention to the lyrics. God was reminding me of truths and speaking to my heart. It moved me to tears as I sorted through the years of memories that surfaced. I cried for lost relationships and mourned connections I never really received from my dad, my mom, my husband, his sister, and my in-laws.

The hurts—caused and felt—surfaced. I understood I had to let them all go. I had to let go of the expectations of relationships in the way I needed and wanted them. God clearly showed me he absolutely and completely loved me. In His love, I had the capacity to love my dad, mom, husband, sister-in-law, and in-laws. Through Christ's love in me, I can love others.

This profound truth hit my heart hard: they do not have to love or care for me. I do not need to try to receive their love—God loves me— that's enough, more than enough. God was healing me.

I pulled my old journals out and began reading through them. Reading page after page from past entries, I noticed I was learning about myself, starting to like, love, understand, and forgive myself—to offer myself compassion and mercy. I saw patterns, and my heart's desires were consistent throughout the years. Damien and I struggled for many years. I was alone while married for years. I was alone and crying on New Year's Eve and several other occasions. There was no account of special, romantic moments with my husband. Except for that one great show of effort on Damien's part when he planned a night out for us inspired by my favorite movie at the time, *Pretty Woman.* He encouraged me to buy a long red dress and then took me out to a fine dining establishment in a rented long white limousine. The evening was wonderful from what I remember. Sadly, too few of these moments were enjoyed. Great love, compassion, and gentleness rose for the little girl— Georgette. I was lost for too long, hurting and misunderstood. I had spent most of my life wanting to be loved, noticed, and cared for.

Despite having a family that loved me, the best they could and having parents who raised their children the best they could, my emotional life was hard even before my marriage. In one childhood entry, I wondered if I should ask my mother why she hated me. She often yelled at me with such anger. Another entry reads, "She wants Daddy to beat me (my parents spanked us at times) because I was saying I did not want to be two-faced about God and being a Christian. Being one way at home and another way at church." I would ask to stay home from church, but it was not an option. Decades later, I would learn more about my mom's struggle with depression and mental health, stemming from her troubled childhood and the abuse she received from her mother.

I know my parents loved me, and I love them, but our relationship was unhealthy for as long as I can remember. For many reasons, I desperately wanted to leave home. Parental control, more freedom, and wanting to experience life fostered a desire to flee. I rushed to get married to Damien because I thought marriage would bring me happiness. The journey through my journal confirmed I had a relationship with God throughout the years. It wasn't always how it should have been, but I wanted to be what He wanted me to be. I desired to be better and do better. I also realized how long I'd struggled with self-hatred, a negative body image, and depression. That season was ending. God was working to heal and deliver me. He showed me how special He thinks I am.

God knew my heart and always had. He knows all of me—my innermost being—through and through. If Damien has a different perception of me, even if he thinks poorly of me or doesn't care to know me or my heart, God loves me. Whether my father and mother have their views about me or don't always think fondly of me, it doesn't change God's love for me. God's love for me doesn't hinge on Damien's family's beliefs or thoughts about me. The God of the universe, the God who created me, KNOWS ME. He has always been with me and has always LOVED me. His love for me is all that matters.

* * *

It wasn't long after my separation became official, with my husband no longer living with me when God prompted me to seek a support group and counseling. He did this a few times throughout the years, all instrumental in helping me gain a new perspective. I needed to take the time to acknowledge all the bad and remember the good memories, experiences, and lessons learned. I learned to focus on what God says about it rather than what others say or what I may have perceived as truth. Perspectives are full of flaws; they are limited. My personal perspectives link to my individual experiences, understanding, and abilities. I needed to ask for God's perspective in all situations. I also needed courage to be myself. "The beauty of finding the courage to face our fears and become ourselves is that everyone eventually wins" (Sue Patton Thoele). I learned I was emotionally dependent. "Emotional dependence is the opposite of emotional strength. It means needing to have others to survive, wanting others to 'do it for us,' and dependent on others to give us our self-image, make our decisions, and take care of us financially. When we are emotionally dependent, we look to others for our happiness, our concept of 'self,' and our emotional well-being. Such vulnerability necessitates a search for and dependence on outer support for a sense of our own worth" (Sue Patton Thoele). Sue's words described my own state of emotions. "Fear—of not being loved, of abandonment, of being thought to be selfish—is the main thing that keeps us vulnerable and bound in the chains of emotional dependence." No wonder I did not move away for college upon my high school graduation, and why I felt I could not speak my truth.

Community, primarily my spiritual church family, played a substantial role in my healing and growth journey. Friendships were critical in helping me authentically live as I learned to serve and receive love from others. Friendships impact the heart in unbelievable ways. This was true for me in all of the rich friendships God made possible for me. First, my friendship with my neighbors Tom, Julia, Kacey, and Lara. Second, I have friendships within my Ladies Bible Study group, especially with my friends Lisa and Tracy, whom I remain close with. Long-lasting friendships are indeed a treasure. Not only is it a treat to witness another's life, but it's an extreme privilege to witness personal healing and growth and new seasons encompassing many prayers that have come to life! These friendships are like diamonds in every sense, from the formation process to the glorious splendor and shine gleaned between friends who bore witness to the struggles overcome. To this day, there's no get-together where we do not acknowledge all God has done in our hearts and lives. Shared gratitude is such a gift! Much like a Swedish Proverb explains, "Shared joy is a double joy; shared sorrow is half a sorrow."

Help came many times through divine appointments or synchronicity in an unplanned special connection. On one such divine appointment, I met a Christian financial advisor, Al Soricelli. He took the time to sit down with me and understand my financial situation, providing guidance on moving forward. I received excellent advice and encouragement. Hope filled my heart where despair had once been.

Finances would be an ongoing and challenging circumstance throughout my single-mom years. There were moments of feeling okay, feeling burdens lift, and even noticing a little sunshine. These financial challenges were where I could have fallen prey to choosing bitterness. But I decided to be better in the area primarily responsible for many of my tears and burdens that were heavy as a wool blanket. God provided relief and ease on multiple occasions, including fun heart gifts just because God loves me and loved to bless me with things that brought a smile and joy to my heart. "And so, we know and rely on the love God has for us. God is love. Whoever lives in love lives in God, and God in them" (1 John 4:16 NIV).

JEWELS

No matter the crisis, and there were many, God helped me through it. Coming home to find an eviction notice on the door was not fun, but it brought me to new levels of faith and trust in my relationship with God and made way for connecting with others—my struggle with finances required courage and strength. I navigated extreme fear and darkness at times that brought forth extensive anxiety. It was from the very depth of this darkness and fear that deep-abiding faith emerged. During this season of struggle, I began to understand how God takes care of me. Jessie and I experienced first-hand care, love, and restoration, repeatedly. No one could convince me God, Jesus, and the Holy Spirit were not real when our precise needs were provided for every single day.

My steadfast faith originated here in brokenness and despair. Beauty and delight ever-so-gently sprang forth within me. The fibers in my being held Heaven. The work of the Potter is a sight to behold.

Forgiveness is a vital component to living better and not bitter. At the beginning of my healing journey, the work was overwhelming. I started from the beginning and addressed the whole picture, from the past to the present. For me, the forgiveness process happened in stages and required a daily heart check-up. God brought books and programs into my life that helped me learn how to work through the steps of forgiveness for each person I needed to forgive.

Significant healing and freedom began when I released the past hurts to God. "Let go and let God" became a daily mantra. The "Our Father Prayer" was, and still is, a foundation, "forgive us as we forgive others." I had to acknowledge I needed a lot of forgiveness. I could not afford to hold onto grudges. Plus, the more I forgave, the more joy I experienced.

While I was busy forgiving others, God revealed that forgiveness for oneself was part of the process. I had been unable to forgive myself for all I had done and all I had perceived to have done in my failed marriage. God revealed, yes, some were my responsibility, but others were not. Are we not going to forgive ourselves when He has already done so, putting us in a position of disobedience to this command "to forgive"? He had my attention. I included myself in the work.

Once forgiveness work began, God's two most important commands, love God and love others (Matthew 22:37-40), became the next apparent nugget of wisdom to receive and put into practice. Love your enemies and yourself is a life-long practice. Learning how to love myself and others, especially those who treated me poorly or rejected me, is quite a feat. But it is possible.

The choice of becoming bitter or better was indeed up to me. No one has the power to control my thoughts or beliefs about myself or my life and circumstances. "We create our own world by our thoughts. And thus, we make our own Heaven, our own Hell" (Swami Muktananda). Allowing resentment to fester is choosing the bitter path, and healing won't happen there. It is harder to face the hurts and practice forgiveness consciously, but it is worth every arduous step. Resentment blocks joy. My ex-husband carried resentment toward me and refused to drop it. Resenting me was his choice and his responsibility. I had my own choices to make and own, and I chose joy. What about you? You, too, have your choices to make and own.

Embrace the possible. Drop what no longer serves you on your path to healing and wholeness. Risk stepping out of your safe places. Sue Patton Thoel said, "When we settle for less in order to feel safe, we always feel sorry. If we compromise our dreams, limiting ourselves with negative ideas gleaned in childhood or adulthood; if we accept that it's useless to ask for what we want and need; if we believe lack is safer than abundance, our lives will close around us like a safe but suffocating blanket. We do need security, but security can be purchased at too high a price. Security obtained at the expense of exhilarating, creative growth and change merely strangles us. Surely, the caterpillar feels secure in its cocoon, but when it emerges, it needs to unfold its wings and risk flight." Sue also shared that fears can be transformed just by changing your thoughts; your fears are not you, and you are not them. You can diminish them and act in spite of them.

You deserve this gift of beginning. The path of bitterness blocks you from soaring. You do not have to know your dream in its entirety, and it's okay not to know what your future holds for you or how to move toward your dreams. Follow your curiosity. Unforgiveness and resentment do not serve well. I don't know about you, but I desperately needed forgiveness at the beginning of my healing journey, and honestly, I still need forgiveness daily.

Prayer and meditation unlock the shackles that bind you. Jon Kabat-Zinn advises us to recognize the bloom of the present moment, to try going outside and looking at the stars, at the moon, or at the dawning light. Feel the air, the cold, the warmth. Seriously, we can drop this junk. Your mental and emotional freedom is a great cause to pursue with passion.

"Let all bitterness, and wrath, and anger, and clamor, and evil speaking, be put away from you, with all malice; and be ye kind to one another, tenderhearted, forgiving one another, even as God for Christ's sake hath forgiven you" (Ephesians 4:31-32 KJV). "Put away from you" is a verb, an action God tells us to do. Golly, even as we have been forgiven. Each of us will always need forgiveness.

I urge you to hunt for an uplifting community, church, and counseling. God has beautiful plans and surprises for you, even in the desert of loss and brokenness. He promises to once again deal marvelously with His people, wondrously marvelous (Isaiah 29:14). Through God's touches and fun surprises, He serendipitously scattered His love throughout my life, especially during sad, hard seasons. Be on the lookout for God's serendipity in your life.

May bravery allow your heart to be vulnerable and open to new friendships. "We always see our worst selves, our most vulnerable selves. We need someone else to get close enough to tell us we're wrong—someone we trust" (David Levithan). Quality, trusted people are the exact mirrors needed. My friends were my heart family before my family of birth experienced healing. Your heart will blossom from treasured friendships. You can choose your own way. You can choose joy.

The last of the human freedoms—to choose one's attitude in any given set of circumstances, to choose one's own way.

—VICTOR FRANKL

CHAPTER 8

Reflection and Revelation

"Life can only be understood backwards;
but it must be lived forwards."

—SØREN KIERKEGAARD

What happened?

Why did the relationship end?

Who am I?

As humans, we seem to get stuck on the obvious pain factors, and at first, this was the heartache of rejection and abandonment. Why did this individual no longer love me or want me? I blamed myself initially because I possessed no self-worth and did not understand my value, nor did I know the truth of what constitutes a whole, healthy relationship. There are two parties equally responsible for the condition of the relationship. Too much time was spent on idealizing the man and the relationship. No one person or relationship is perfect. I heard a TED Talk, "How to Fix a Broken Heart," given by Psychologist Guy Winch (April 2017), that explained why I experienced such emotional pain and why I struggled to face the truth of the marriage. Winch shared how "brain studies have shown that the withdrawal of romantic love activates the same mechanisms in our brain that get activated when addicts are withdrawing from substances like cocaine or opioids" (Fisher et al., "Intense, Passionate, Romantic Love: A Natural Addiction? How the Fields that Investigate Romance and Substance Abuse Can Inform Each Other." Frontiers in Psychology (2016): 7:687). When the marriage was ending, I went through withdrawal. But since the initial plan was to give the marriage another shot, I still had hope, that is, until I realized my ex-husband's behavior only portrayed his negative feelings toward me, and my heart relived the rejection repeatedly.

God's rescue plan is holistic in nature. Taking time to reflect on who I have been, who I was, the people in my life, and my life experiences were vital in moving forward with meaning and purpose toward healing. This included uncovering family history and understanding family dynamics and how they related to me. There is generally a reason for what we do and why we do it. God revealed to me how learning about my family background, personalities, dynamics, past pains, sins, etc., matters. They bring meaningful truths that lead to revelation and freedom.

Being driven by my insecurities guided many negative choices in my life, like my early marriage. Being needy and empty is not the ideal time to enter a relationship, and as an eighteen-year-old, I did not possess these truths or understand generational patterns. I married to be loved and to experience physical intimacy. There were scars on my soul caused by instability in the home, significant loss, rejection, dramatic change, and personal limitations. My insecurity resulted from the way I coped rather than healed and robbed me of the ability to accept and receive love, made me a fool on many occasions, caused me to overcommunicate, be overcontrolling, made me feel not good enough, made me do things I didn't want to do, caused me to accept things as normal that aren't, caused me to overcompensate (frequent hairspray applications to keep hair looking good all of the time, honor student, overachiever to name a few examples), made me settle (in everything), and even gave me a hang-up to going to the bathroom in a public restroom!

After my divorce and during my single years, especially early in the healing journey, I needed to be wanted and accepted. It's not the ideal state to meet someone with good character and godly intentions.

I also learned from Sue Patton Theole that I was a "responsibility sponge" who assumed responsibility for other people's happiness. I thought if I was nice and kind and pleased everyone, everything and everyone would be okay. Not rocking the boat or sticking out as a people-pleaser would no longer serve me.

* * *

When I started the process of making amends with anyone I may have hurt or wronged in the past, the path God had revealed to me, I wrote a letter to each person. Those letters, which I read to my family at Thanksgiving, were an empowering exercise that let me heal more deeply with myself and those I cared about.

We repent, and God saves. When I cried out to God from the floor of my closet, broken, desperate, and alone, He responded immediately. He set forth the rescue, which included reconciliation, first between Him and me and, eventually, with others. Restoration in all realms also began spiritually, emotionally, mentally, and physically. Reading the Bible daily and becoming familiar with various scriptures were instrumental to this process.

"As for me, this is my promise to them, says the Lord, my Holy Spirit shall not leave them, and they shall want the good and hate the wrong, they and their children and their children's children forever" (Isaiah 59:21).

The story of Job in the Bible, his significant loss and grief, resonated with me during my season of complete loss. I faced losing the dream, love, family, romance, and the future I'd hoped for. It was the hope of a total restoration that kept me from giving up, and it was something that God orchestrated for me personally, even if it didn't look like I'd imagined. God's restoration in my life has surpassed my wildest expectations. I came to experience the promises from Isaiah 59:21 in many ways as the years went by. It is true. God forgives, heals, and restores, but this doesn't mean He returns to you what was lost. It means He restores as it should have been, even better, perfected for you and fulfilling His desires for you, which are only good.

I knew throughout the reflection, revelation, and restoration process something grander was in the works. "Be glad, O people of Zion, rejoice in the Lord your God ... I will repay you for the years the locusts have eaten (Joel 2:23, 25 NIV)."

Remember not the former things, nor consider the things of old. Behold, I am doing a new thing; now it springs forth, do you not perceive it? I will make a way in the wilderness and rivers in the desert.

—ISAIAH 43:18-19 NIV

* * *

I continued to answer altar calls on my knees in prayer, and God met me there. Physically walking up, kneeling, and presenting my heart in utter humility was a holy moment. His love is there for us all the time, but in those hushed and holy moments, I believe He moved on my behalf in a special way.

One thing I have learned is to respond when my heart feels tweaked. One Sunday morning, after a touching sermon, I did just that. I felt guided in my prayers to figuratively place the Cross of Christ on my heart and on the divorce, allowing it to cover the years gone by, back to the beginning of all the hurts, rejections, and failures. I was now open to receiving God's miracles, love, and blessings. It was a powerful experience.

As I learned to respond to God's altar nudges, I also began a rhythm of waking up early to pray. In the very early hours of one Friday morning, I experienced something miraculous. While praying and crying out to God, I felt led to my journals. I went straight to the one from when I was twelve. I had written about circumstances involving my parents, an incident that had occurred that left me finding out things about my father I never wished I had learned. I read where he was yelling at us, and we were crying. I read about how I did not like him at that time due to being hurt. (This hurt would later turn into rebellion and disrespect.)

After reading this entry, I prayed and asked God to forgive my dad and me and heal us. This experience of learning about my father's mistakes in his marriage occurred around the same time I found Jesus and right before I met my first husband. It was the moment God revealed to me that the root of my unforgiveness began and started to change my heart.

Things with my father began to get better. God orchestrated details for a unique gift as my father's birthday approached. During prayer time, I remembered a CD I had purchased, *Butterfly Kisses and Bedtime Prayers.* It was a particular song God wanted me to hear: "Butterfly Kisses," written by Bob Carlisle. This song makes me cry each time I listen. I wasn't sure how to do it, but I knew what God asked me to do.

God wanted me to write my dad a letter with words from my heart, sharing how I love him, asking for his forgiveness, and offering forgiveness, including a copy of the CD in the letter. Communicating with my parents from an emotional place was not familiar to me or to them.

My parents certainly didn't learn emotionally healthy ways from their parents. My mother was hated by her own mother, and her father left the family to marry a much younger woman. Dad's parents survived WWII concentration camps, and his mom did not want children but made a deal with her husband that she would raise them until they were a certain age, and then they would be his responsibility. He did not live up to the agreement. There was no communication in the home, which could be because my grandparents did not learn English very well. I had heard that my dad received his first hug from his father when he married my mom.

The letter to my dad was ten pages long. Our family met for dinner at a favorite spot, Perkins Restaurant & Bakery. I don't remember how he liked his gift or if he ever said anything about it, but I did what God asked me to do, and I was thankful I shared my heart.

JEWELS

God is constantly giving us His version of butterfly kisses. No matter what your journey is, what your losses or sorrows are, when you walk together with Him, He will start healing you layer by layer from the outside to the inside. Beauty and delight from your brokenness and despair become greater and greater. I walked the path and can testify that the great news is His healing never stops. He continually brings you to destiny moments until you experience more joy than you could have imagined.

During a difficult conversation with my mom, she shared a profound truth: to get to the other side of anything, you must go through the mud, the yuk, junk, painful, hard stuff. We had been discussing our hurts, what we each held on to, and how we felt. It was hard, but it allowed for truth to be shared; the tears flowed, and a chance for our relationship to heal began. Every healthy relationship at times includes seasons of walking through the mud. Relationships need nurturing, care, and maintenance. Sometimes, feelings get hurt, misunderstandings occur, and maybe offenses are taken and buried, which only hurts the relationship. Conducting heart checks periodically is wise. Asking another their perspective on the health of a relationship can be scary, but in doing so, concerns can be addressed easily. Walking through the mud is a conflict resolution for heart matters. Keeping one's heart tidy ensures less mud to wade through when seeking relationship restoration.

Loving relationships remain loving when the hard stuff is addressed. Conflict avoidance is never a good idea. The weight of mud can become heavy beyond handling, and the relationship will break. If I cared, I would walk through the mud to bring every issue to the surface and allow God's love and light to clean and refresh my heart.

Have you started journaling yet? As you have learned from my own story, journaling was a powerful tool for me and can help you as well. The words in your journal reveal great truths about everything: you, your life, your circumstances, your relationships, your dreams, past, present, and future. What better way to reflect on your past and current circumstances and receive revelation from God to your heart. What an excellent place to compose your own "reality" list of the person's traits and relationship memories that caused your heartache and to prevent the idealization of this individual and relationship.

Review your childhood and understand all the people involved and how each of them, along with specific circumstances, helped shape who you became. Pouring out your heart to God is a beautiful process and a lovely journey to add to your life, and you will always have it. When you draw near to God (James 1:4), He draws near to you. God is my hero. He is my greatest love. May you also come to know this great love that is trustworthy.

God knows where you are insecure, and He will not leave you as He finds you. "As a father has compassion on his children, so the Lord has compassion on those who fear him; for he knows how we are formed, he remembers that we are dust" (Psalm 103:13-14 NIV). What fills your love tank? Dr. Kevin Leman explains, "An empty love tank is often a contributing factor for marital breakdown—also juvenile delinquency. If you want to have a successful, happy life and a healthy home, and you want to be the "new you" you dream of becoming, it's vital that you are able to identify your own love language and learn to speak your loved one's as well."

I want, by understanding myself, to understand others. I want to be all that I am capable of becoming... This all sounds very strenuous and serious. But now that I have wrestled with it, it's no longer so. I feel happy—deep down. All is well.

—KATHERINE MANSFIELD

SECTION II

The Wilderness

It is the Lord who goes before you. He will be
with you; he will not leave you or forsake
you. Do not fear or be dismayed.

—DEUTERONOMY 31:8

CHAPTER 9

Bloom Where Planted

"It is a crime to despair. We must learn to draw from misfortune the means of future strength."

—WINSTON CHURCHILL

The phrase "bloom where you are planted" is credited to the Bishop of Geneva, Saint Francis de Sales (1567-1622), and it seemed to be popping up everywhere in my life. I even bought a tiny watering can with the saying on it, taking the reminder that blooming where I was was a possibility. This gave me hope.

I recollect how, most days, I actively tried to deny or avoid my current circumstances. That season of my life was full of hardships I had no desire to accept. God made it clear, though, it was a time when the work was acceptance, acclimations, and adjustments galore. With His help, I bloomed right where I was. Most days, I had no desire to do so because I was too busy praying for another rescue; for my ship to sail away toward better circumstances. But this was not to be. And I learned how beautiful blooming where you are planted could be.

God was with me throughout the whole process. Charlotte Beck said,

"Life always gives us exactly the teacher we need at every moment. This includes every mosquito, every misfortune, every red light, every traffic

jam, every obnoxious supervisor (or employee), every illness, every loss,
every moment of joy, or depression, every addiction, every piece of gar-
bage, every breath——every moment is a teacher."

God orchestrated my steps with divine appointments lovingly sprin-
kled wherever needed.

As an insurance agent-to-be, I was on the hunt for leads to potential
new accounts, so during lunch, less than four months away from our final
divorce court hearing, I walked into Lucio's Restaurant to talk business.
It went great. They shared with me when their insurance policy was due
to be renewed and about a recent claim that was not covered. God was
so good. I had been crying out to Him many times, especially recently,
about my ability only to pay the rent, car payment, and car insurance, but
nothing else.

I cried, "Oh, God. Send your miracles, funds for the other bills, an eye
appointment, groceries, and everything else I have stacking up." I asked
Him if I should get another job, but I didn't want to go that route because
my days were already full. I was studying for the Property & Casualty
Insurance exam and was hoping to go from being a customer service representative to a licensed insurance producer, which would be a step up for
me professionally with more opportunities for financial gain in the future.

Well, one of the owners of Lucio's, Janine, asked if I wanted a part-
time job and offered to work around my schedule, so I took it. With an extra three days of work, it provided me with some extra money. My schedule
worked perfectly with Jessie's. I still got to see her enough during the week!
It wasn't as much time as either of us would've liked, but God worked it
out in a way that still allowed me to spend precious time with her!

I remember how this young man, who I shall refer to as "Boy Chef,"
was infatuated with me. As I struggled over my approaching divorce, his
attention and kind treatment did much to heal my self-esteem. I know I

have said this before, but it's true and amazing how every person I met and got to know became a part of the healing process.

Significant healing occurred after a Disney trip. The owner had invited all of us to go to Disney and stay in his condominium. Three of us went with him. Boy Chef was one, and he insisted on paying my way. Disney with the boys was a day of fun but hampered because I had to stop in every bathroom we passed to freshen up and ensure I looked okay, which didn't go unnoticed.

My "brothers" from Lucio's asked me about it and had a "sit down" with me and told me how pretty I was and that I didn't need to go into the bathroom constantly to check on my hair. I asked God for healing and delivery of my insecurity. I prayed that I would no longer need to use hairspray. I wanted to be natural and free and comfortable with myself. I was starting to feel and see some of what God was doing inside me.

I figuratively laid down my hairspray at the cross during my time with God. God and I both knew what "hairspray" meant for me. Like a security blanket, I always carried a big bottle, and my constant need to respray, no matter where I was, represented deep inner emptiness, insecurity, and low self-worth.

God's an awesome God. I am one of His miracles! It's wonderful; I am amazed at the transformation, the changes. I am happy and full of joy and peace.

Our Lucio's clan had become a mini family.

* * *

Housing was the first change under the separation/divorce knife. I was fortunate to stay in our apartment while Damien moved out. The whole affair continued to bring sadness. There was just never enough money, and I considered moving somewhere with lower rent.

I even made an appointment and met with a man to see the area he had for rent in his home. Everything was shared. No real privacy. No real place for my daughter. Again, I was trying to jump from the hardship. I was already living in the crème da la crème of available housing. I even tried to apply for welfare and was denied. My biggest takeaway? Home is where the heart is. My daughter and I loved our home, and we enjoyed being there, where it was filled with love, peace, and laughter—just more of the miraculous gifts God bestowed upon us.

Jessie also loved her school and thrived … until she didn't. The divorce took a toll on her, and her grades dropped to a dangerous level, enough that the school principal arranged a meeting with me. After the divorce, I decided to keep her in the school and use the child support money to help pay her tuition. The intentions were good. This was her other family, and she was loved there by many and needed as much love and support as possible. She didn't need to be uprooted again.

But when it became apparent that she would need to repeat a grade if I kept her there, I investigated the public school system again. After much prayer and discussion with friends, I returned Jessie to the public school system. It was a game-changer. Her grades immediately improved, and she made new friends.

Finances were something we continued to struggle with. While the child support helped toward her education, in the long run, my daughter's greatest desire was to spend time with her mommy. The price for me to work a few jobs to keep a roof over my head and pay bills was costly, a price that left my heart scarred. Moving her to public school sooner would have helped the overall financial situation. My 20/20 hindsight can hopefully help others now. Housing should have been the priority, then education. The way to have gone was to provide a stable home and routine where my daughter and I could enjoy free time and hobbies together.

9 | Bloom Where Planted

Press forward, press hard, and keep pressing until you break through the barrier that has stumped you.

—JEFF O'LEARY

* * *

When I stood before the divorce court judge, it was accepted practice for items agreed upon during the mediation sessions to be included in the final divorce papers. Before the judge signed off, she kept asking me if I was sure I wished to agree with the child support agreed upon, for it was a low figure. I was too scared to say I wasn't okay with it. I had no idea what a fair amount was, and I was too afraid to anger Damien and jeopardize a potential future friendship.

Whenever I tried to review the income compared to our total expenses, it never made sense. God provided. Jessie and I never went hungry, but it was on a survival basis for a while. Ramen noodles were a staple in our house. We shopped at the Dollar Store and day-old bakery items were a go-to for yummy goodies. There was no money for extra items and no room for crisis. Someone should have told "crisis" this because crisis still came, primarily car troubles. This put us over every single time. I did make the choice to treat Jessie and me to Olive Garden sometimes. She would order her mini pizza with olives, taking them off to put on all her fingers.

A vision remained within my heart of my future self, filled with confidence. God worked on me from the inside out. His ways are mysterious, higher than our ways. He showed me I have worth. As the past died off, the present opened beautifully into the glorious future God had in store for me and my daughter.

Looking back from one Christmas to the next, my circumstances did not change, but I did. I possessed more inner peace and strength from

Christ. When I asked God why I was still alone, He answered me through a devotional book I came across, *The Desert of Solitude*.

"But when God, who set me apart from birth and called me by his grace, was pleased to reveal his Son in me ... I did not consult any man ... but I went immediately into Arabia and later returned to Damascus" (Galatians 1:15-17). "Distancing yourself from something that once held your heart can be a kind of withdrawing into the desert of solitude where desires can be purified. It's a way of detaching your desire from the magnetic pulls of this world in order to attach it more firmly to Christ." And this is exactly what had occurred. "Oh, how great is your goodness to those who publicly declare that you will rescue them. For you have stored up great blessings for those, who trust and reverence you" (Psalm 31:19)!

Financial fear overwhelmed me greatly, to the point that I went to a pawn shop and inquired on the value of my engagement ring in a desperate effort to obtain funds to pay bills. They were only offering $250.00. It was agreed I would be able to get more if I sold it myself. At a later time, rent was due, and I did not have the funds, so to avoid eviction, I knew it was time to sell this ring, one I'd hoped to pass down to my daughter, but having a roof over our head mattered more. I ended up talking to a man I'd met at a part time job, and when I explained my situation, he asked how much my rent was. I can't remember if that was the amount he offered me for the ring or pretty darn close to it, but what a gracious act.

God heard my prayers. My first paycheck from my new insurance agency job as an insurance producer brought a surprise and a smile! The understanding was I would be working and earning commissions, but my paycheck included a base salary. They decided to provide it to help me.

New friendships blossomed: with Wil, a personal trainer at my new gym, Adrian from my insurance class, and Mike, my neighbor, and letter writing continued with my teenage youth group friend Greg. As I was pleasantly distracted, prayers for my new husband began.

◢ JEWELS ◗

Bloom where planted, my dear one. Life does bring many hardships and challenges, but these circumstances are used to bring new insights and truths into our lives. God uses tough stuff to guide us and lead us and uses change to move us onto new paths. What we believe to be a detour was the exact change in direction we needed.

Troubles are used to reveal valuable information. Difficulties and trials have a way of helping us grow and, crazily enough, sometimes protecting us. Yes, we desire to heal from the pain caused by others. Maybe consider sitting in your pain and reflecting on what happened and your feelings. What are all your options? I know I have suggested this a few times already, but good advice bears repeating. Maybe now it is time to reach out for help from others. You do not have to go it alone.

If I had not taken time to pray and reflect, I most definitely would have put my daughter and myself in unsafe places and probably would have increased our pain. Navigating options for our children can be quite difficult, and the failure of my marriage placed that burden on my shoulders alone and within my heart. There is so much loss; the hope is to reduce the amount of loss and change.

Wisdom helps us see through emotions and brings clarity to make better decisions. Seek financial counsel as soon as possible to gain this wisdom from professionals. Spending most of your income on a private school may not be the most logical, especially if your income is limited. Personally, hearing other people I admired tell me I was doing the best I could gave me huge relief. Financial follies can be avoided. Know the state of your bank account and credit card balances. Making priority for time and fun with your children is a gift that will keep on giving. Whatever you do, find healthy responsible ways to treat yourselves.

As the past dies off, the present opens beautifully into the glorious future. Remember, no matter where you find yourself today, you will not be there forever. Seasons come, and seasons go. God hears every single prayer. What season do you find yourself in today? The Rescue season is quite dramatic and noticeable, but the Wilderness season sneaks up on you. During times of reflection and review, I noticed the changes that had occurred in my life, within me and outside of me, as portrayed through our schedule and activities. Know where you are. Observe the details and plan celebrations for the areas where you are blooming.

May you decide not to jump ship of what is your current life for a perceived better ship. "The more you seek security, the less of it you have. But the more you seek opportunity, the more likely it is that you will achieve the security that you desire" (Brian Tracy).

Deal with your difficulties. Joyce Meyer reminds us, "We simply cannot keep trying to escape or avoid situations that are difficult. Anytime we run from a situation, we can almost be sure we will have to go back and face it, or something very similar, at a later time in our lives" (*Never Give Up*). Running from adversity may rob you of the exact buffing required to do a specific healing or development you need.

Every difficulty I encountered was instrumental in shaping me to be who I am today. No problem is ever good, but God promises to work all things out for our good (Romans 8:28). You'll see! Pray for discernment and trust the Creator's process with all troubles encountered. Keep going. Stand strong. Your roots are strong, and they go deep, which means you have what you need within you to thrive, to never give up.

You can bloom where planted, my friend. You also can rip up any roots God has rooted. He gave us free will, and our journey through life is a partnership involving our daily surrender to His will and His ways. He does not force us to obey His Word or follow Him. Our relationship involves a two-way commitment. He remains committed. Are you? Are you committed to yourself as well? Are you committed to seeing this through? You are worth it! Commitment to trusting God's process in your life guarantees you'll live out the purpose of your life and experience your dreams fulfilled.

Harriet Beecher Stowe stated, "When you get into a tight place, and everything goes against you, till it seems as though you could not hold on a minute longer, never give up then, for that is just the place and time that the tide will turn." The tide will turn, and your bloom will be stunning.

If I were asked to give what I consider the single most useful bit of advice for all humanity it would be this: Expect trouble as an inevitable part of life, and when it comes, hold your head high, look it squarely in the eye and say, "I will be bigger than you. You cannot defeat me."

—ANN LANDERS

CHAPTER 10
Single Motherhood

*"Sometimes the poorest man leaves his children
the richest inheritance."*

—RUTH E. RENKEL

Embracing my new singleness had been a struggle. I had no desire to be alone. Sadly, as I was amid my own healing and surviving, so was my daughter. Jessie had been going through the grief phases along with me. As much as I didn't want to be single or a single mother, she also had no desire to be without her father. She was forced into a whole new season of life as a little girl and didn't have the coping skills to understand or adapt.

A mom's greatest desire is to protect and care for her children. My baby's heart was broken, and I could do nothing about it. I was unable to protect her from every negative situation. My heart was already broken, and this added another layer of brokenness to me. I was not whole, and now, the responsibility of filling the absent role of "father" was overwhelming. Her "birth father," as my daughter now refers to him, was not involved in her daily life. He kept the divorce agreement visitation schedule for a while, but that faded. The weekly visits became fewer over the years, and the overnight stays stopped completely.

It became clear that God's protective hand was over Jessie through those visitation changes. In one instance, a stepbrother shot and killed two men over a drug deal and was sentenced to prison.

Parenting challenges arose almost daily, it seemed. I did not know how to respond or what to do much of the time. Here is where relying on my faith and God helped me and saved me. God utilized my love of reading to bring new insight into my life at just the right moment. Stories encouraged, inspired, and taught me. My church family modeled life for me in numerous ways, and I had the ability to ask questions, and in my prayer group, not only were heart matters discussed at length, but how to raise our children properly was prayed on.

"It is easier to build strong children than to repair broken adults" (Frederick Douglass). I came to realize I was parenting from a place of brokenness, and as new truths were revealed about myself, I knew seeking help to change would benefit me, but more so, it would benefit my daughter and future generations. My own mom and dad understood some of the parenting mistakes made by their own parents and intentionally made different parenting choices for their kids. I, too, did not wish for Jessie to go through similar painful ordeals that I encountered, and this meant I had to change. And change I did with God's guidance and aid. Obedience, humility, and a willingness to be vulnerable were required for the breakthroughs received. There were occasions when I would feel embarrassed and bad about myself and my perceived lack of ability, skills, or emotional well-being, especially when I witnessed other moms who seemed to be perfectly put-together. But these moms had their own problems, which I learned about after getting to know them better. Isabel Rojas Lopez said, "You see, we are so often caught up with a person's outer shell and make assumptions on what we see that we miss the sign and the red flags."

* * *

Every morning, Jessie and I would sit and do devotions together, and I would pray the "Priestly Blessing" over her: "The Lord bless you and keep you; the Lord make his face shine on you and be gracious to you; the Lord turn his face toward you and give you peace" (Numbers 6:24-26). Some mornings, we said this on the go as we grabbed breakfast at Burger King. (Jessie loved their French toast sticks.) A relationship with God is one of the greatest blessings I could ever pass on to my daughter. I could not give this to her, but I could live my relationship with God out in front of her. My words and deeds mattered most. How I lived is what she would remember. I made choices with this in mind.

The most important thing to my daughter was her parents; myself and her father. Toys or electronic gadgets would not have filled her heart or spirit. Jessie desired to spend time with both of us. Since the pool was next to the laundry room, most times, she and I would bring down our laundry, throw it into the wash, and walk right over to the pool. We would finish the laundry while enjoying ourselves out in the sunshine—a perfect set-up!

Barnes & Noble Booksellers, Morningside Library, the Dollar Store, Dunkin Donuts, and Olive Garden became part of our traditions and routines. Adding these places for us to spend time together brought us fun and great joy. Watching my daughter play at the beach and hearing her laugh cheered my heart. I loved observing her and felt mighty blessed to be her mom.

She was prayed over daily. My faith and relationship with God were what I trusted in. Through the years, I experienced His hands in my and my daughter's lives. We were His. He had us. Jessie seeing me face down on the floor praying with my Bible laid out next to me was a regular occurrence. One time, she got on the floor and prayed with me. She learned how to pray and talk to God by watching and hearing me. God and I had daily moments throughout the day, every day. I poured out my heart through spoken words, written words in my journal, and worship through songs or tears.

There were always financial worries and life concerns written about in my journal, which were my prayers. One great testimony to my prayer life came when Jessie was older. She shared with me she never knew of our struggles or worries and didn't feel we were poor. God balanced us and provided and gave us great ideas for fun adventures.

God's love and my daughter's love for me were the wind beneath my wings. So cliché, yes, but the truth. Their love kept me and inspired me to live a good life. My daughter's love was a pure gift. Her words "I love you, Mommy" on a yellow Post-it were a treasure and encouraged me. I still have all the little notes she would leave for me, even the sad one where she informed me she was praying I could be home more.

* * *

Throughout the years at our Pinewood Pointe Apartment community, I was often reminded of the miracle of God's placing Jessie and me here. Our pool was the hub where most residents spent a lot of time, especially the children. My daughter enjoyed her friendships and playing with the other children in the water. Little Maya, Tyler, Mandy, and Jordania were a few regular friends. And our spiritual community enriched her in many ways. She benefited from relationships with Christ-followers of all ages. Being known and valued by so many did our self-esteem well.

🔥 JEWELS 🌑

Single motherhood is a vital role; there is much at stake for us and our children. Our response to life's challenges and hurts dictates the future. We must decide if we will be bitter or better and if we will bloom where planted. Dear one, you have what it takes to be a phoenix rising from the ashes. Our every word and deed will show the way.

Creating a new mission statement for your new family will serve as a guide and an inspiration. Do it together. Dream big. Write it out, place it in a frame, and hang it where everyone can see it daily. In her blog, "How and Why to Write a Family Mission Statement," Sarah Conway writes that creating a family mission statement helps foster a sense of belonging in your family, which builds resilience in our children. This helps them develop healthy self-esteem and self-identity and instills the confidence they need to manage challenges. As parents, we make a way for a positive family culture to develop, and this occurs when we become intentional about setting clear guidelines and clearly stating what matters most to us as a family. What are your values? What do you stand for and expect from each other? What are your favorite places to be as a family?

May I share something with you, from this momma's heart to yours? When scheduling and planning out your days, plan everything around your children. I know it's hard to believe during crazy days, but your time with them is short. Take many photos to capture all your moments. Quality time with you is what they prefer, trust me.

Sharing meals together could be a continual source of enjoyment and entertainment as you navigate life together, helping each of you to remain connected and bonded. Each family member could have a special role to play. Roles can be assigned or written on a piece of paper, and monthly draws occur to determine who does what. Some roles could include meal planning, table preparations, cleanup crew, etc. Holding family game nights or adding consistent routines that incorporate new traditions desired by your kids could be glue helping all to stay strong together.

As tempting as it may be, try not to entrust your children's minds and hearts to technology. TV and digital devices are a super convenient way to keep one's kids occupied, but this has lasting effects, and research shows they are not good. Things have changed a lot over these past decades. It is even more urgent for parents to be diligent and know what their kids are doing and watching. Each of us needs community and conversation and real face-to-face, in-person relationships. This is what feeds us and what we thrive in. Finding opportunities where children can play together and where you connect with others is essential.

You will have overwhelming, tiring moments, but you are not alone. God provides help and rest. "The Lord replied, 'My Presence will go with you, and I will give you rest" (Exodus 33:14 NIV). And know this: single parents can be really good parents. God can change our circumstances no matter how bad things may have been. We have hope in Him. "May the God of hope fill you with all joy and peace as you trust in him, so that you may overflow with hope by the power of the Holy Spirit" (Romans 15:13 NIV).

Your kids will also have overwhelming moments and fear. Get to know your children. They may need to talk about what they are feeling, or they may need you to ask them how they are doing and provide listening ears and open arms. Hurting kids act out at times, and older ones are especially prone to be rebellious, but God can change and soften the hardest of hearts. You may not love your child's behavior, but you love them, and God loves them more than you, always. No situation with your child is hopeless. "What is impossible with men is possible with God" (Luke 18:27 NIV).

Awareness of our own brokenness and what we are unconsciously spreading to our children unnecessarily will allow us to determine and intend to do better and differently. You can take ownership of how your brokenness hurt yourself and others, and you can start today. From this place, you can move forward, parenting from genuine love and graciousness. The next step is yours to take. Make some changes! Have fun doing it, and involve your children when it makes sense. My daughter and I would play loud music and create a celebration when our rooms and closets needed organizing. Maybe your family can create new traditions around the areas of concern or struggle. Ask your children for their ideas and solutions.

The most powerful two words spoken are life-changing: "I'm sorry." Parents are not perfect people. Did you react poorly? Make a mistake? Acknowledge it, say you're sorry, and ask for forgiveness. Ask for a "do-over." Give grace and receive grace. You all deserve it. Modeling greatness is the supreme parenting act.

No matter what comes your way, you can handle it. No matter what comes your child's way, you both can handle it. No goal is impossible, and every obstacle is surmountable.

Our life is frittered away by detail ... Simplify, Simplify, Simplify! ... Simplicity of life and elevation of purpose.

—HENRY DAVID THOREAU

CHAPTER 11

Praying and Planting

"May God grant your heart's desires and make all your plans succeed."

—PSALM 20:4

Praying had become my love language with God. I have been praying or talking to God since I was a little girl. My faith began in the Catholic denomination, where I learned about confession and received communion. In later years, our family found God in a Pentecostal church, which brought us to the "faith" churches.

Praying can refer to someone saying words to a deity, people praying for divine guidance or their loved ones. When tragic circumstances occur, my first response is to "pray" about the situation and for the people involved. At times, especially in the Catholic faith, I pray through specially written prayers like the "Lord's Prayer" or the "Our Father" prayer, which Jesus used to teach the disciples how to pray.

In Matthew 6:9-13 (NKJV), I learned that Jesus instructed his followers not to pray publicly (or for show) but to go to a private place and pray to the Father. Jesus said: "In this manner, therefore, pray: 'Our Father in heaven, hallowed be your name. Your kingdom come. Your will be done on earth as it is in heaven. Give us this day our daily bread. And forgive us our debts, as we forgive our debtors. And do not lead us into temptation, but deliver us from the evil one.'"

When I prayed this prayer, I made sure I prayed the ending verse 13a (NKJV); "For yours is the kingdom and the power and the glory, forever. Amen"

Eileen Flanagan shared with her readers in her book, *The Wisdom to Know the Difference*, a different version from the later popular version of the Serenity Prayer credited to a Protestant theologian, Reinhold Niebuhr that I, to this day, include in my prayer toolbox. He included this version in a sermon he delivered during World War II:

God, give us grace

To accept with serenity the things that cannot be changed,

Courage to change the things that should be changed,

And wisdom to distinguish the one from the other.

Prayer is something I can do in a group or by myself. Heartfelt prayers availed much. They were not for show. This was my heart-to-heart moment with the creator of the universe, my Abba Father. Prayer became something special after a relationship formed between God and me. For me, prayers started with uttering words to the God I believed in but could not see, hoping He would hear me. Prayers became much more meaningful after I invited Jesus into my heart, and especially after my cry from the bottom of my closet floor.

Prayer is a supernatural life force. In the good times and bad, prayer is my primary connection to my Heavenly Father, including Jesus and the Holy Spirit. I witnessed God's responses to my prayers and His personal touches. I was not alone. God heard me. I had proof in the pages of my journal. My prayer time with God refreshed me and helped to guide me in all facets of my life, including single parenting. Prayer helped me to see "that of God in every person," a Quaker belief, and increased my anticipation for "sparks of the Divine," as Rabbi Erin Hirsh calls it, in my daily living.

* * *

I was abandoned, some emotionally and some physically, by those closest to me. Loneliness and despair seemed to have no desire to leave me, but the more I poured my heart out to God, the more I experienced His presence and responses. Faith esteem bubbled up and took over in areas where despair had taken up residence. As love increased, love and faith had more power and ownership of my head and heart.

I thought about my new job with an assisted living organization and was profoundly moved by the organization's name, "TenderCare Services." I had the opportunity to watch tender care occur through the hands of others and gained insight into what it means to be the hands and feet of God, to provide hope and healing with tender care. I realized again how tenderly God cares for us and for me and Jessie. Receiving this part-time job was no accident. The extra money was extremely beneficial, and I learned firsthand how to care for others tenderly. I believe God wanted me to know and be encouraged by His continual tender care for us.

* * *

God hears heart whispers, loud rants, or silent tears. I was encouraged to pray, for my prayers were intertwined with the divine and were my hope for the future. I was in a real relationship with someone who saw me, someone I mattered to, and someone who delighted in me.

"The Lord your God is in your midst, a mighty one who will save; he will rejoice over you with gladness; he will quiet you by his love; he will exalt over you with loud singing" (Zephaniah 3:17 ESV). His love for me allowed trust and hope to grow within me. He did not always respond to all I had asked for, but He responded with what I needed the most. Because I knew He cared, I humbly received and learned to wait on Him. He is, after all, the potter, and I was the clay, as Isaiah 64:8 (ESV) says; "But now, O Lord, you are our Father; we are the clay, and you are our potter; we are all the work of your hand." "Has the potter no right over the clay, to make out of the same lump one vessel for honorable use and another for dishonorable use?" (Romans 9:21 ESV). God was creating His masterpiece. I learned to appreciate all His touches, even the rougher ones.

My prayers for a second chance at love intensified during my long, single mom years. God, the Potter, was preparing me for the day I would meet the man He selected for me and my daughter. A man after God's heart, as I desired. He would need to show me what that looked like because, up to this point, I really had no idea what type of man this would be.

* * *

I don't have adequate words to describe what occurred on April 30, 2001, within my heart, soul, and spirit—but I'll try. It was the dawn of a new day and the setting of the old. I was listening to music while praying and worshipping God. Prayers for my dreams and passions started off softly but steadily increased in fervor. In my innermost, I desired for what I knew to be the real Georgette to become a reality and not just to reside only in the dream realm.

My love of history, art, music, people, places, thoughts, ideas, relationships, then and now, flooded my heart. A strong sense of knowing rose within—an epic epiphany. I will step into the "waters" of Indian River Community College (now Indian River State College (IRSC)) tomorrow to register as a new student. I could not see myself as an insurance producer in the years ahead. But I knew I strongly desired to help people as I had been helped. I didn't know how I would do it, but I knew Father God would work it out.

I earned my associate degree in liberal arts and Bachelor of Arts degree in Education as a single mom, and later, a master's degree in human services marriage and family counseling. Since I was a woman who loved learning, I needed to realize that a good match for me would be someone on a similar level: educated, intelligent, and an avid reader.

My humanities professor was a man around my age, handsome, intelligent, and wore a tweed jacket and dress shoes. While I was impressed, he was married and not available. Each day in class, while I was observing and listening to him teach, one day, the truth burst. *Why couldn't I find someone like this and have an educated husband who likes learning and discussing new things?*

I wanted someone who could have intelligent conversations about people and life. I needed someone interesting. Why did it have to be someone who never read or had anything interesting to discuss? Why did I need to be with someone who only worked and was never available? It didn't! Bam!

I gauged my spiritual and emotional health by noticing the types of people I hung around or desired to be with. Anytime God revealed a new truth about me or life in general, I added those new truths to my prayers. This included prayers for what God had promised for me today and tomorrow.

Planting seeds of prayer pertained to all facets of my life, even work. My new job as an insurance agent with a local agency had become a great challenge. It was hard enough to generate leads and receive requests for quotes on new policies, but when I finally received a request for a quote, especially with business liability, the agency did not have decent insurance markets to place the business with. Then came a potential client with a large account. My commission would be a beautiful blessing if I could secure this account. I had faith and reliance on God. He was my only hope.

After a few months of prayer and working on this prospective account, the news came that the organization decided to go with our agency. This was my first sizeable commercial account, which meant my first nice-sized commission check.

A new me, a new car, and a new year had begun. Our old car did its last awful thing on US 1, a major federal highway. I fondly remember this experience because even with car troubles, God showed up wonderfully! I had called Enterprise to rent a car and met a wonderful girl named Lisa who needed some encouragement that day. We planned to get together, and I invited her to our Tuesday Bible Study. When I returned the car, I found out that Enterprise actually sells cars and ended up trading my Mercury Cougar for a 2000 Mitsubishi Galant, V4, with 20,000 miles. That car helped us save on gas, and Jessica and I loved it.

* * *

On one of my nights working at Lucio's Restaurant, I shared my experiences with everyone from a Friday night. After I shared, my co-worker John led me to the truth God wanted me to hear.

He said, "Georgette, do you want to date or to get married?"

His question felt so profound! I was considering dating again, even though I knew that the men I had been considering were not husband material. Why waste my time and put myself in a challenging circumstance? Yes, I got lonely at times. Yes, I would like to be treated well and feel seen and attractive. But my genuine desire was to wait for God's best and meet that educated and interesting man who loved God wholeheartedly. I asked

God to forgive me for losing proper focus. I was not going to take the wrong path. In Daniel 1:8, to keep from defiling himself, Daniel resolved not to eat the royal meat or drink the royal wine. Like Daniel, I was determined in my heart to decline any dinner invitation from a guy I just met.

* * *

Prayer provides protection and discernment. Jacob obeyed and found his wife (Genesis 28-29). I needed to obey God to find my husband! My daughter and I made prayer lists, listing our dreams, short-term needs, and hopes.

02-06-01, Georgette's Prayer List, In God We Trust

1. Financial blessings/miracles, all debt paid, student loan, IRSC, Capital One, Higher income/salary

2. Lose weight, all excess

3. More quality/free time with Jessie to do fun things: plays, operas, day trips, movies, dinners, weekend trips, vacations

4. Piano for lessons

5. Marriage: "Heaven on earth" romance, loves God with all his heart

6. To be organized and disciplined, a Proverbs 31 woman

7. College or courses to learn more, improve skills

8. To be able to go shopping for new clothes and shoes and feel and look pretty

9. Dental work

10. Eyeglasses

11. BNI networking group

12. Fulfilling career

13. REST

Jessica's Prayer List

1. Daddy

2. Van

3. House with stairs

4. Never leave Wetherbee Elementary

5. New printer, ink for the printer

6. Bigger TV, new table

7. Bigger house

8. More time at movie theater

9. More time with Leah

10. See Mommy more on Friday and Saturday nights

11. Get a dog

12. New clothes, new shoes

13. Get on the Principal's Honor Roll

14. New living room

15. New bedroom, newer computer!!

16. Vickie comes over

17. Bigger bed

18. Behave more

19. Improve more

20. More knowledge

21. Bookshelf for books

My mommy's heart hurt when I read her prayer for "see Mommy more." Creating those lists provided good bonding moments for us and provided a powerful way to model prayer for my daughter as we learned about faith, trusting in God, and how to wait on God. We also got to see how creative He was in answering our prayers and how He took care of every detail, big or small. Prayers were not only the seeds we planted for our current circumstances to help our future circumstances take shape, but prayers were the foundation we laid down for our lives. Prayers were the glue that bound it all together.

Praying with a purpose was included in the painting on the canvas process. Sowing as many prayer seeds as possible was our goal. Prayers were living prayers. They were continuous and evolving. "Let those who are wise understand these things ... The paths of the Lord are true and right, and righteous people live by walking in them" (Hosea 14:9 NLT). Praying helped my daughter and I to develop intimate relationships with God, Jesus, and the Holy Spirit. When we prayed, we became heart-to-heart with the Father. In those prayers and prayer times, we begin to feel His presence and gain an understanding of who He is and who we are, and this is where we gain powerful insight into where we came from and where God may be leading us to. Prayers were and are the beginning of everything, including healing and development. God saw me (Genesis 16:13). God showed me His approval and made my efforts successful (Psalm 90:17). My prayer sessions became quite special. Here I came as myself, as I was on any given day, happy or sad. I would spend time thanking God for all He was doing, for all He had done, and for all He was going to do in the days and years to come. I played Christian music and sang to God in worship.

Other times, I started off with reading my Bible and reading Psalms and then prayed about everything on my heart. And I mean everything. Here was where the tears would begin if that were the case. After I shared my whole heart and mind, I would continue reading through my Bible, parts of the Old Testament and the New Testament, with a chapter of Proverbs for the day. Afterward, I sat or lay quietly with God. Here is where I gleaned the treasures and jewels God had for me. I would be better after every single session with God. It was through those moments I experienced transformation.

Praying helped me to live in the now. My prayers included prayers asking God to help me remain content as a single. That meant no more waiting for a special someone before I could live and be. My conversations and journaling with God helped me learn to be present with who I was and content with what I had already.

After sharing my heart with God regarding new culinary desires, one day, while shopping at Publix, I felt moved to splurge, buying more than just the necessities. Usually, those purchases included champagne or wine, Godiva ice cream, muenster cheese, grapefruit, romaine lettuce, red potatoes, or the two-person serving of tiramisu.

Other ideas generated from my sessions were how I would start walking in the mornings as I continued going to the gym for my health and emotional well-being. I wanted to eat better and bless and encourage everyone I met as I smiled and shared kind words. I wrote out my affirmations and declarations of truth for myself. There was power in this. There's now a whole arena set aside just for self-development and affirmations. So much research backing up the *Law of Attraction*, what I believed and focused on would grow and come to me, good or bad!

God revealed to me that my prayers came from my heart, and He placed them there along with my dreams. My prayers evolved as I did as a person and as a woman and mom, daughter, sister, and friend. These actions were what guided my ship. They gave me direction to seek counseling, prayer from others, ideas on how to serve God and others better, how to forgive, what to forgive, how to be, and what to pursue, all generated through my prayers and journaling.

* * *

As a planner, I often prayed about the same thing repeatedly and researched how to do something I was interested in instead of going out and trying it. Kate Wheeler said, "True adventures start with desire, an inclination to enter the unknown." And because I came from an insecure background, afraid of loss or rejection, stepping into this sacred space of the unknown was something I put off until the pain of not stepping into this space became too unbearable.

Talking to God about my life was one thing but becoming something or someone required me to do new things and make choices to bring about change. Every day, a conscious choice is necessary to shed the old—whatever "the old" means for us—old issues, old guilt, old patterns, old responses, old resentments, old rivalries. We no longer have the luxury of wallowing in what has held us back; this is the emotional baggage we're supposed to be getting rid of. For me, going to the gym and taking time to walk helped me eat better and lose weight. Through my time with God and the books He brought into my life, I learned much about myself, who I was, and what I was created to be and do. God even revealed my heart's passions and interests, which included my love of the ocean, flowers, chocolate, and art! Quiet moments like this were never wasted moments. I received ideas to look further into the community to see what was out there.

Attending plays and musicals brought immense joy. I could not always afford to purchase tickets, but God creatively hooked his daughter up repeatedly. To this day, I receive a free ticket to the Palm Beach International Art, Antique, and Jewelry showcase every year. God made this special treat possible for me, and now, it's a tradition. Walking through this showcase and seeing such beautiful art with such history and value is a heaven-on-earth moment.

I followed the different playhouses and their schedules, which was how I discovered Jim Brickman! I love piano music, and when I was younger, I took lessons. My biggest regret later in life was stopping these lessons during my teenage years, especially when I discovered how musically adept I was. I was thrilled to be able to attend one of his concerts at the Lyric Theater in Downtown Stuart. Of course, I had to purchase one of his CDs. Then, I wondered if my new husband would be a musician!

Praying together continued for Jessica and me. As a mom, I loved sharing heart with my daughter. I loved even more how humble, vulnerable, and open she and I were with God.

JEWELS

God can grant your heart's desires and make all your plans succeed (Psalm 20:4). He does this in partnership with you, with your heart all in for Him and your desires entrusted to Him. Your Bible guides every desire worth having and provides practical steps to pursue the passions God places within you. Prayer helps you to understand His Word and provides discernment on what He has planned for you and how to interpret His scriptures throughout your life.

Beautiful soul, you are never alone. God cares about your heart, life, family, circumstances, anxieties, and fears. "Rejoice in the Lord always. I will say it again: Rejoice! Let your gentleness be evident to all. The Lord is near. Do not be anxious about anything, but in every situation, by prayer and petition, with thanksgiving, present your requests to God. And the peace of God, which transcends all understanding, will guard your hearts and your minds in Christ Jesus" (Philippians 4:4-7 NIV). Dennis Merritt Jones's mindfulness practice tells us, "The next time you feel lost in life and without clear direction, first remember that, in truth, you can never really be lost."

God provides visual examples of how He desires us to live and what we can look forward to as we follow Him.

Remember in Chapter 4, I shared my altar experience after going up to pray? When I opened my eyes, the guest speaker, Jamie Parsons, was on his knees. This visual stayed with me. I learned to pray and ask God for a man who prayed and was humble enough to pray on his knees. This type of man would directly take life's issues and concerns to God. There is safety and love in this kind of behavior exhibited. Relationships benefit.

God will provide his followers with all sorts of illustrations in ways our hearts understand. God restores, including restoring what we may have lost through generational repeats. What we may not have known better about, God will take the time to educate us after healing us, so we make new choices and decisions that bring freedom and joy.

In *The Life You've Always Wanted* by John Ortberg, he writes several profound statements; "the possibility of transformation is the essence of hope;" "The primary goal of spiritual life is human transformation;" and "The first goal of spiritual life is the reclamation of the human race. It's morphing time." In my walk with the Lord, I not only learned change was possible for me, but I experienced many changes which morphed into a complete transformation of my inner being, which then became visible as exhibited by the joy of the Lord and my growing desire to love and help other people, and I became a person who found it easy doing so.

What do you say about yourself daily? Compose your personal affirmations along with your favorite scriptures to refer to daily. I collect powerful, inspiring quotes and affirmations that I refer to often. I love how Sue Patton Thoele describes positive thinking and affirmations. She tells us that "clean thoughts are what we need to have in order to grow closer to our own souls." You are the only one who can clean up your thoughts. Sue suggests creating "flower sentences." Seed sentences are self-affirming and supportive. One of my flower sentences is, "I am a unique, loved, valued, fabulous woman of God." Sue's "SEE" acronym helps us to start liking, admiring, and loving ourselves; "Savor Excellence Everyday."

Consider including the Our Father's Prayer (Matthew 6:9-13) and the Jabez Prayer as outlined in 1 Chronicles 4:9-10 (NIV): "Jabez was more honorable than his brothers. His mother had named him Jabez, saying, 'I gave birth to him in pain.' Jabez cried out to the God of Israel, 'Oh, that you would bless me and enlarge my territory! Let your hand be with me, and keep me from harm so that I will be free from pain.' And God granted his request."

If you have children, I invite you to pray together as a family every morning and every evening before bed. Compose your prayer lists together, and watch and see how God moves in your hearts and home! I encourage you to participate in small groups for discipleship opportunities and to find ways to do life with other Christians.

Prayers define your relationship with God and how you enjoy His intimacy. Life is brighter and lighter when your heart overflows with prayers in God's presence. During your prayer time, you become aware of God's presence and know how much He loves you without a shadow of a doubt. There are many jewels within you to yet be discovered. There is a vast new land for you to conquer with your Abba Father. Beauty and delight reside in your prayers.

The greatest gift you can give to yourself and everyone you care about is daily continuous alone time with God. There is no price to express the value stemming from your God heart-to-heart moments. Prayer is our jewel to all of life's beauty and treasures. God desires you and I to be in communion with Him daily through prayer as we celebrate our days and share our concerns. "Rejoice always, pray without ceasing, give thanks in all circumstances; for this is the will of God in Christ Jesus for you" (1 Thessalonians 5:16-18). D.L. Moody said, "Every great movement of God can be traced to a kneeling figure." I know for certain how impactful my prayer life was and remains so for me and for my family. My life story is the proof!

The reality is, my prayers don't change God. But, I am convinced prayer changes me. Praying boldly boots me out of that stale place of religious habit into authentic connection with God Himself.

—LYSA TERKEURST

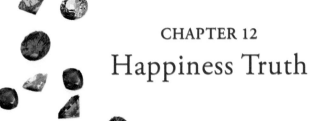

CHAPTER 12
Happiness Truth

*"The power of finding beauty in the humblest things
makes home happy and life lovely."*

—LOUISA MAY ALCOTT

There is growth and development in the seasons of grieving. A lot of this occurred while I was kicking, screaming, crying, and begging for it to all stop. But I would never have become who I am today or gleaned all the spiritual nuggets received without having experienced the pain and sorrow. My growth from grief started when I cried out for help.

God created the universe. His ways are higher than our ways. He loves creating and educating His loved ones. There was forgiveness and restoration galore throughout my grieving season. Bittersweet betterment was continuous, including God's miracle of bringing my destiny decision full circle.

I made the wrong destiny decision when I decided not to go to college after graduating from high school and to get married instead. God sometimes allows us to see the results of our choices. I knew that fear guided my decision.

I loved how God brought education back around for me. Even though the two-and-a-half years were tough, they were thoroughly enjoyable.

Sweet betterment occurred daily in my classes and the orchestration of our other life responsibilities. God helped us maneuver the schedules of my many jobs and Jessica's schooling. When it was time to make changes or leave a job, He guided the whole process.

Every semester, with new books and classes, brought tremendous pride and excitement. Education was a part of my healing. The bittersweet betterment occurred during my transition from the old to the new, from death to a brand-new life. How I arrived there was an interesting process, lovingly directed by God Himself.

* * *

Each day, my levels of gratitude were growing by leaps and bounds. Some days, my thankfulness list seemed endless. My blessings were vast with relationships, shelter, food, clothing, and community. Melody Beattie spoke truthful words when she said, "Gratitude unlocks the fullness of life. It turns what we have into enough, and more. It turns denial into acceptance, chaos to order, and confusion to clarity. It can turn a meal into a feast, a house into a home, a stranger into a friend. Gratitude makes sense of our past, brings peace for today, and creates a vision for tomorrow." My daughter and I possessed abundant peace and joy and were thankful and grateful for our home and life.

The realization of how much God delivered me from settled in, deliverance from my own Egypt. I was set free from depression caused by the long New England winters, loneliness, feelings of low self-worth, rejection, abandonment, and feeling stuck in uncontrollable circumstances.

God revealed the various generational repeats in my life. Divorce, depression, and discouragement, to name a few, were like daily shackles holding me back. His journey of healing is like no other. He accepted me, adopted me as I was, and loved me unconditionally, with forgiveness extended as often as needed in utter compassion.

Some things needed to die—old belief systems and relationships that no longer served me well. Placing limitations on dysfunctional thinking and living is paramount. God challenged all these old and inaccurate belief systems. He repeatedly showed me my worth and value until His truth started to sink in. I learned that what I had perceived as accurate as a little girl or young adolescent in response to other people's behavior many times had nothing to do with me. It had to do with other people's issues and the hurts they themselves carried. Understanding this helped me to shift past beliefs of what other individuals thought of me to what God believed of me.

Happiness is not having what you want, it is wanting what you have.

—ANONYMOUS

* * *

Those single years with just Jesus, Jessie, and me were some of the happiest of my life. This does not mean there weren't moments of grief and sorrow, but despite the hardships, I discovered joy in my relationship with Jesus. Through my errors, mistakes, and struggles, I learned what was really important. Meeting another man to be loved was not the solution to my problems and was not the key to my happiness.

When fresh in my loss, I was not in a good state of mind. Emotional pain clogged my sight and discernment. I wouldn't have chosen baptism by fire, but the outcome and results experienced couldn't have occurred any other way. Suffering was where my junk transformed into jewels; my brokenness and despair became beauty and delight. It's challenging to explain, but when you know, you know. All my dark and depressing struggles changed me from the inside out.

As I've mentioned previously, during my separation, a new neighbor started paying attention to me. In short, a grown man, older than I was, who had a little girl, was himself separated (still married) and living with his parents, riding his bike. There were some pretty giant, bright red flags waving.

During this season of my life, I did not notice these giant red flags—not one. In the depths of despair, people do not see the right colors. This man had many past girlfriends, two of whom got pregnant, and he encouraged them to have abortions.

Why the bike? He was arrested for driving drunk and went to jail. The DUI involved him really hurting a woman. OK, now, my eyes have started to open a little. After jail, he got caught with beer again, lost his license, and rode a bike as his sole method of transportation. A great catch, right?! I was vulnerable, raw, and desperate to be wanted. Any attention paid to me from a male seemed to be good, which is a scary place to be, and predators sense this.

No one, absolutely no one, can love like God can. This new truth slammed into me as I was reading Habakkuk 3:17-19 (NLT), "Though the fig tree does not bud and there are no grapes on the vines, though the olive crop fails and the fields produce no food, though there are no sheep in the pen and no cattle in the stalls, yet I will rejoice in the Lord, I will be joyful in God my Savior. The Sovereign Lord is my strength; he makes my feet like the feet of a deer; he enables me to tread on the heights." My happiness does not come directly from a romantic relationship. Events and circumstances surrounding me should not dictate my feelings. Apostle Paul expressed his thoughts about true happiness: "In everything we do, we show that we are true ministers of God. We patiently endure troubles and hardships and calamities of every kind. We have been beaten, been put in prison, faced angry mobs, worked to exhaustion, endured sleepless nights, and gone without food. We prove ourselves by our purity, our understanding, our patience, our kindness, by the Holy Spirit within us, and by our sincere love. We faithfully preach the truth. God's power is working in us. We use the weapons of righteousness in the right hand for attack and the left hand for defense. We serve God whether people honor us or despise us, whether they slander us or praise us. We are honest, but they call us impostors. We are ignored, even though we are well known. We live close to death, but we are still alive. We have been beaten, but we have not been killed. Our hearts ache, but at the same time we have the joy of the Lord. We are poor, but we give rich spiritual gifts to others. We own nothing and yet we enjoy everything" (2nd Corinthians 4-10 NLT).

I remain in awe of Paul. After being stripped, beaten with rods, and thrown in jail, he still worshipped God.

Mother Teresa once stated that, "God is joy, joy is prayer. Joy is a sign of generosity. When you are full of joy, you move faster, and you want to go about doing good to everyone. Joy is a sign of union with God—of God's presence." This was the joy I desired ultimately.

I immediately repented for seeking happiness from earthly, temporary plans or circumstances, especially with seeking happiness from the attention of others. The joy of the Lord is what I really needed, one that didn't come from my relationships or circumstances. Becoming like a little teapot, pouring love onto others, brought utter joy to my heart. Quality time with my daughter, and doing activities together brought happiness.

"I waited patiently for the Lord; and He inclined to me, and heard my cry. He also brought me up out of a horrible pit. Out of the miry clay. And set my feet upon a rock, and established my steps. He has put a new song in my mouth …" (Psalm 40:1-3).

To daily meditate on all God had done within me and for me humbles me every single time, and smiles come. There is substance to this joy, and that is the type of happiness I seek.

* * *

Parenting is a role God himself places moms and dads in. I did my best with who I was and what I was capable of. Being a good role model for my daughter was my priority, especially with resolutions I made in private. I understood the relevance of how I lived my life in public and in private matters would impact my daughter's future. I was working hard to plant good seeds for future generational repeats to be for good. I valued our relationship and her heart more than anything (after my relationship with God, of course). And notes like this brought the greatest cheer.

Nov. 26, 2001

Dear Mommy,

I love you so much you are very precious to me. God blessed me with you. I am very thankful for you. I just don't know what to say. You are a love to me. I love you very much.

Love Jessica

It was a win-win to keep my focus on God and on my daughter. Children are treasures. As God's child, I, too, was a treasure worth discovering and protecting. I could choose to see and receive His love and believe in myself. And I did.

 **JEWELS**

God breaks the chains that bind us as He delivers us from our Egypt. God desires a "new you" as He did for me. Whatever you are carrying, you can give it to God. You, too, will experience your metamorphosis. And it is not a pretty or comfortable process, but a necessary one.

Maybe going back to college is not your desire or meant for you, but find out what is. What have you always wanted to do? What are you excited about? If you could do something for free, what would it be?

The rescue season is fresh in the midst of loss or brokenness, when you can't fully trust yourself. Daring not to date might possibly be a priority, for everyone's sake. This is the time to soak in God, soak in all the love and tenderness He brings to you through everything and everyone around you. This is the time for demolition and rebuilding, tearing up the old foundation, and laying gorgeous, beautiful, strong, and sturdy stones for your future.

God will use people to help us heal and teach us new truths. He will use potential partners to provide examples of what we are worthy of and what no longer fits. God will provide visual, real-life circumstances to show us what is possible.

Listening to what the experts say about dating after the end of a relationship, especially as a parent, may be hard, especially in the beginning when your heart is hurt and raw. Needing and receiving love during painful seasons is a heightened desire. When you are not quite ready, dating can be risky because it increases the odds of attracting the wrong type of person into your life. Your kids need you more than ever during life transitions. God brought love to my heart in a variety of delightful ways. He can do the same for you.

The love from and for our children is paramount during the healing and grieving stages. Love that is balanced and healthy. Parents must be cautious and aware of the dangers of enmeshment where boundaries get crossed and roles and expectations become confused. This is a common occurrence in families of divorce, where the proper boundaries between parent and child get blurred, and a parent may rely on the support of their children or be afraid to set forth proper parental boundaries and structure with fear of loss of love. Parents may try too hard to become friends with their children in lieu of parenting.

Once your feet are on more stable ground, during the wilderness season, you may consider putting your toes in the water by participating in group activities to meet new people, men and women, in group settings and develop new healthy relationships with the goal of friendships. In the beginning, surrounding yourself with emotionally healthy people is key to your own healing journey. Then, later, as your own wounds have healed and you are more balanced, as you enter the promised land season, you can pay even more attention to the various types of individuals you come across, for this may be the season your head and heart are finally ready and healthy enough to meet new people for future partner potential.

"Hope begins in the dark, the stubborn hope that if you just show up and try to do the right thing, the dawn will come. You wait and watch and work; you don't give up."

—ANNE LAMOTT

CHAPTER 13

Thrive in Tribe

"Tell your story. Shout it. Write it. Whisper it if you have to. But tell it. Some won't understand it. Some will outright reject it. But many will thank you for it. And then the most magical thing will happen. One by one, voices will start whispering, 'Me, too.' And your tribe will gather. And you will never feel alone again."

—L.R. KNOST

One day during prayer, I discovered the truth and reality of my life. I actually had a real life, one where I was discovering joy and laughter, along with new interests and meeting new friends. God showed me how I thrived best in a tribe.

Community was where I found my purpose played out. I learned of my greater role in life and what I brought to the table for my local community, business partners, city, state, and country. As I show up for others, they show up for me. However, my involvement within the community at large did not occur until after God established a spiritual community for me first. From that foundation, I felt led and confident enough to volunteer for our St. Lucie County Chamber as an Ambassador. Being around other professionals taught me so much and helped me increase my personal confidence. Later, involvement in a Toastmasters Organization brought additional knowledge and growth.

Spiritual community became the greatest blessing in my life to this very day. I did not know how special my church family would become until many years later. When strangers come together and follow Jesus and do life together, something magical occurs. Hearts are shared. Trust is built. Safety is found. There is nothing like being with sisters and brothers in Christ who have known you from the ugly beginning of your faith walk to the transformation that occurs through the years afterward. Bearing witness to the growth of others and having others bear witness to your own development is a heaven-on-earth gift. This is junk to jewels played out over and over again, impacting individual lives and our world in valuable ways. I was blessed to have been placed within a church family God deemed perfect for me and my daughter and has been for twenty years. With sadness, after the loss of my mother, God uprooted us from this church family because the season here had ended. I grieved this as a loss, but only so much because when God desires to uproot us and move us, He has His reasons, and I would always prefer to be exactly where God wishes my heart to be. He has never done me wrong on this. God uprooted Abraham. "The LORD had said to Abram, 'Go from your country, your people, and your father's household to the land I will show you. I will make you into a great nation, and I will bless you; I will make your name great, and you will be a blessing. I will bless those who bless you, and whoever curses you I will curse; and all peoples on earth will be blessed through you.'" (Genesis 12:1-3 NIV). For good cause, too. God was saving a nation and a future of people that included me. God had a plan for my life, and there are times He moves us to a new place or territory for His plan to be fulfilled.

My heart greatly values my season within this church family, many of whom I remain connected to. Having a strong spiritual momma and sisters and brothers speaking life into you and surrounding you and offering words of wisdom and help when needed is priceless. I would not have made it after my divorce without them. I would not be the woman of God I am today without them. This was a love of a whole new level I had never experienced before. On my first Easter in this church family, I was invited by a new friend, Lori Gagne, to her family's home for a meal. It was the best Easter I had experienced in my new two-way relationship with God. The spirit was there, and my heart was loved and refreshed. My daughter and I were seen and counted as one of the members of this family of God. We were enjoyed, and we mattered. How beautiful is that?

In the beginning, during the transition from marriage to separation before the divorce, God guided me to participate in the Evangelism Explosion group. God took the time to teach me His Word, and He shared His heart with me. God desired to know me and for me to know Him fully. He used other people to help me. This group and the people in it at the time were used to bring God's truth to my heart and help my daughter and me. I learned the roots of the gospel and how to share it best with others.

Sometimes I found myself participating in things from an invitation from someone. By saying yes, I was able to find out what I loved or did not love and what I was good at even. I was invited to join the church's softball team. Even though I was nervous about meeting new people and didn't know if I would even be any good, I said yes. This was the first miracle God did for me. God brought me full circle back to a destiny decision I had made from fear and shame. You see, back in high school, at the end of freshman year, I was going to try out for the lady's softball team. I made it to the very last day of preparations for tryouts but chickened out and didn't go to the tryout. I was embarrassed about my appearance, experienced shame, and was petrified to fail in public in front of others. I felt so ugly I just couldn't show up. I believe God wanted to use this sport and team to begin healing within me from these very issues. God can do anything, including reversing destiny decisions that altered one's life's path. God has the power to place individuals on an entirely different path, one filled with adventure and surprises. Yes, the path may include pain and sorrows, but it will also include massive joy, love, and laughter. This group of men and women were so kind to my daughter and me. We enjoyed wonderful fellowship after each of the games and came to know each other. This was the first group of people I got to know, and then it blossomed from there. And guess what? I was pretty good at the game. My body was built for sports, and my spirit of competitiveness belonged in this arena.

* * *

Giving back most definitely means giving my time, talent, and energy and sharing my heart with others. But this also incorporated financial giving, starting with tithes and offerings, and supporting others as situations came to my attention. For me, there may not be any leftover finances after paying bills or never being able to to pay the necessary bills completely. Here is where it got hard. God showed me the importance of having faith in this area of my life and trusting in Him. It seemed the more I trusted and the more I tithed and gave, the more He would bring blessings to me in a variety of interesting ways: cash here and there from members in our church, from the Ladies Bible Group, and Christmas gifts from church members for Jessica. God impressed upon me that no matter what my circumstances were, I could focus on giving. I did not have to wait for my own financial increase to do so—I could give from what I had. I immediately started encouraging others more, and I gave a $10 gas gift card to a co-worker who needed help. I sacrificially gave to our special Christmas offering. And you know what? Every time I assessed our financial situation, it made no sense how we were making it, but God was taking care of us.

JEWELS

Dear one, you can trust in God to handle every aspect of you and your children well. "God knows far more about living a life of joy and blessings than we do" (Randy Loubier). He has you.

Your tribe is unique to you. But make no mistake, every prodding and nudge you feel for something, pay attention because God is leading you. Every part of my journey included activities, groups, and organizations, all of which were instruments in additional healing and learning. These tweaks and touches are integral to who we ultimately become. Take time to reflect on your own journey up to this point. Invest in yourself and in your children. When you feed your passions, your life purpose comes to the surface. Keep feeding the fire, and you will be amazed at where you may find yourself. Surround yourself with those who leave you better.

When it's time, your heart will know this, and God will, too. You will grow an interest in serving somewhere. This is good and is the crucial part of your own healing. As we contribute and serve, we find great joy. Your tears, wounds, and pain are never wasted. It is these very things you may have within you later as powerful elements in your ability to make a difference. Helping others has a most profound way of, in the end, actually helping us. "From what we get, we can make a living; what we give, however, makes a life" (Arthur Ashe).

You will have work to complete before you find yourself thriving.

Community is where humility and glory touch.

—HENRI NOUWEN

CHAPTER 14

Uniquely You

*"Decide upon your major definite purpose in life and
then organize all your activities around it."*

—BRIAN TRACY

Once I understood the happiness truth that people or circumstances are not the source of my happiness, I came to realize even deeper truths. The love of God, His love for me, and my love for Him were the actual reality everything else stemmed from. In this knowledge, a new revelation gently took hold. The joy of the Lord is in all I am and do. He created me in His image. My identity was formed within His. God was showing me Himself through His Word and His people and, in doing so, was also revealing who I was and who I was created to be. "But now thus says the Lord, he who created you, O Jacob, he who formed you, O Israel: "Fear not, for I have redeemed you; I have called you by name, you are mine" (Isaiah 43:1 ESV). I was known by name.

His rescue of me and my journey have become the greatest joys of my life, including the hardships. Even now, in my promised land where dreams would come true, I am not immune to trials. Life is a continuous journey, and as I've discovered, the journey from brokenness and despair to beauty and delight seems to play on a loop but with us in different places and life seasons.

The more I learned about God, the more I learned about myself. As the layers of hurt and lies slowly healed and shed, my identity and beauty became more evident. My preferences and passions came to life through the miracles and beauties discovered in daily life.

Nature showed itself as one of the first discoveries. The beachside became my special place with God. Hearing and seeing the vastness of the ocean and the continuous flow of the waves invited childlike wonder to take hold. Oh, the tears cried along the seashore, and later, the heart's rejoicing uttered, there was, and is, nothing like it. Observing the beauty and wonder in nature portrayed the beauty and wonder within me.

God created me and others with a specific purpose to live out. "For I know the plans I have for you," declares the Lord, "plans to prosper you and not to harm you, plans to give you hope and a future (Jeremiah 29:11 NIV)." He was helping me in my discovery process, and knowing my purpose helped me through tough seasons.

And I came to believe it was never too late to begin anew. "Being confident of this, that he who began a good work in you will carry it on to completion until the day of Christ Jesus (Philippians 1:6 NIV)." Even if I felt I messed it up badly, "If we confess our sins, he is faithful and just and will forgive us our sins and purify us from all unrighteousness (1 John 1:9 NIV)." God promises anyone who belongs to Christ has become a new person. "The old life is gone; a new life has begun (2 Corinthians 5:17 NLT)." "Through the Lord's mercies we are not consumed, because His compassions fail not. They are new every morning; great is Your faithfulness (Lamentations 3:22-23)."

My work or career may be my purpose or maybe a part of what prepares me for my God-given purpose. My work experiences included jobs such as: working in a commercial landscape office, errand girl, office manager, customer service representative for a worldwide insurance organization, insurance producer in the insurance industry, running a commercial landscape firm by handling all the office responsibilities, including administrative and pursuing and obtaining new jobs. There were seasons when I worked as a server in the restaurant industry, and I even worked for an assisted living organization. Each of these jobs placed me in different environments, each with unique people and circumstances. There were difficulties to navigate through and relationships to build. God used each assignment, each person to usher in greater capacity to handle hard moments and to ultimately shine for Him. Through the many individuals who crossed paths with me I received valuable life lessons and God's love and favor, even in the midst of hardship or disappointment. My life, I came to understand, was beautiful in the journey, the journey itself held vast treasures, the greatest of which was my heart-to-heart relationship with my creator and our fellowship together in the midst of my every day life. And since God is everywhere and found within others, there were grand adventures to be had every single time I opened my eyes and prepared to enter into a new day. God's purpose was to love me as He transforms me into the likeness and image of His Son, Jesus.

My ultimate purpose was establishing myself in God's ways.

On April 3, 2003, I sought God.

Daddy God,

Be with me now, speak to me—advise and direct in ways I know how to hear and understand. I am sitting outside in the middle of IRCC's campus. Test in math today, speech tonight, still so much work for speech. Lord, do we ever reach a point of 100% knowing ourselves, our purpose, and our destiny? Still so many things about me I would like to improve—things that can be changed. God, why am I here? Who am I in you? What does it really mean for me,

Georgette, now—to BE like Jesus in all I do and all I am? I love you, your world, your beauty, and the birds. Bring me to a higher place in you, more understanding and knowledge. Let me be as you are, being as you purposed for me since the beginning—supernatural, wisdom, confidence, strength. Georgette—your daughter, bold, loving, kind, generous, strong, courageous, consistent, faithful, understanding, patient, knowing, discerning. I need you, Jesus, now and always. I desire YOU above all. Jesus, NOTHING else matters here. Let me know, understand our calling to love you, serve you, and love others. I so desire to be where you are, Lord. Love on me, God. Guide me, talk with me, God. Fill me, Jesus. Touch me, God. Please touch me now. Love me, just you and me now. I sit here in the sunshine, with the entire whole universe, the world around me, me, and you. Show me your mysteries. Who you are. Who we are in you. I seek you. You say if we seek you, we will find you. I desire to be with you now. Please, oh, please. I need you. Something from you, YOU, please God. Bless me now with a word. Touch something. My friend Jesus. My Lord Jesus. I worship you. Love casts out ALL fear. I AM with you.

Georgette, I am your God and your Father. You are special, beautiful, talented, creative, worthy, and valuable. You know me. I am yours; you are unique. My purpose in you is to establish you in my ways.

Father, am I where YOU want me? Do I please you now? Am I right with you?

JUST AS YOU ARE brings me great joy and pleasure.

I felt loved and heard, and I was sure of my ultimate purpose.

This is a tiny snapshot of some of my many heartfelt prayers with my Father God. I poured out my heart through the rescue, the wilderness, and even into the promised land. God and I have a history together. In every season, I seemed to be unsure of myself and insecure in His love for me. As I journeyed through life's seasons, I slowly gained confidence in our love walk. My goal was to be established in God's ways. Through the pages of my journals, the desire to write and share my personal story of how God showed up for me and the good news of how God can show up for others took root. God reassured me through His responses that no matter what season I find myself in, He will be with me and guide me, and His love for me is secure and steadfast. Even as I headed toward my promised land, a land full of unknowns.

∗ ∗ ∗

In the beginning, getting dressed up and going out for drinks with girl-friends brought excitement, prevented me from feeling lonely, and brought great conversations and laughter; ultimately, it delayed my journey toward a better-healed version of myself. I knew I had no desire to meet my new mate in a bar. This would not be the story I shared to the question, "How did you meet each other?" I desired a particular type of man, and the odds of finding him in certain environments were small compared to my living my life fully following my heart's dreams and the leading of the Holy Spirit.

It was important for me to know who a person was and how they impacted me—hindrance or help. If a person inspires and encourages me to be my best authentic self, I could keep them in my circle. If a person seemed to drain all my energy or consistently pressured me to do activities that left me conflicted or convicted, it was seriously time to re-evaluate the relationship and schedule less and less with this person. During the worst of my brokenness, I was happy to be hanging with people who made me laugh and who took me out of my comfort zone to go places and meet new people. But after a while, as my healing progressed, it became evident it was time I moved on. Getting through the days is something not meant to last forever. And that is a good thing. This meant there had been healing and change within me. When I reached a decision in this area, my obvious new thing was to serve and help others by volunteering in our church.

First, my daughter and I volunteered to bring church to assisted living facilities. We joined a team that did this. As a mom, I knew how important this lesson would be for my daughter. Later, I volunteered to assist with teaching Sunday School to the younger kids. Jessica would help me when she wasn't in her own Sunday School class. I was then invited to serve on the Telecare ministry, where we called members or visitors of the church to see how they were doing and if they desired prayer. God would move me into working with our teens in the youth group. My pains were used for a purpose, and this continues to evolve to this day. No pain is ever wasted in God's economy.

JEWELS

No matter where you find yourself, one jewel of wisdom remains: You are unique, and your beauty resides within. Your uniqueness holds the greatest virtues. What is He using to reveal your unique self and beauty within?

Johann von Goethe said, "We are shaped and fashioned by what we love." Jeff O'Leary says it best, "Every journey must have a starting point, and the journey to fulfill God's destiny for your life is no different. Christ's ministry began after His baptism and the inspiring words from heaven, 'This is My beloved Son, in whom I am well pleased' (Matthew 3:17

NKJV).' But immediately He was sent into the desert to fast for forty days and be tempted by the devil. Hardly the way for a king to begin the drive to fulfill His destiny! Yet sometimes even the most auspicious journeys begin with mundane inconveniences and impediments."

Be cautious and aware of who and what you allow in your life. This is a one-of-a-kind season, one that will never be the same again. As you learn your uniqueness and firm up your identity, paying attention to potential hindrances is essential. Hindrances will prevent you from moving forward in your growth and development. They will keep you stuck. You are stuck if you find yourself doing the same old things and experiencing the same old pains, crying about the same issues or circumstances. Something may hinder you from accepting new truths and making the necessary changes. For me, specific environments or habits hindered my progress or set me back in my healing.

After each loss and heartbreak, I imagined a blank canvas. I got to decide how I'd move forward, and journaling was a beautiful part of painting my canvas with purpose. If you have never tried journaling, I highly recommend it. Go and treat yourself to a journal that resonates with you.

Taking what you learned about your identity and uniqueness and adding other information gleaned from books and personality assessments will empower you to not only learn more about yourself but will help you to start taking steps to use this knowledge. During counseling and as part of pre-marital counseling, I participated in taking The Myer-Briggs Type Indicator (MBTI). Also, understanding your love language is eye-opening. This is a game changer for all of your relationships and for that second chance in your future. Gary Chapman's *The Five Love Languages* has been a hit since it was initially published in 1990 and is still being reprinted today. Chapman shares five love languages: words of affirmation, quality time, physical touch, acts of service, and receiving gifts. Each of us has different primary languages with some overlap. Knowing our language and the language of others helps us to have better communication and healthier relationships.

Be courageous to head down new paths, especially the ones God directs your feet toward. Follow your heart. Details arrive only as needed and not a second before. Pursue your heart's dreams continuously. Leo C. Rosten sums up the purpose of life well: "I think the purpose of life is to be useful, to be responsible, to be honorable, to be compassionate. It is, after all, to matter, to count, to stand for something, to have made some difference that you lived at all." Believe you can and claim your confidence. Make a difference.

I have learned this at least by my experiment: that if one advances confidently in the direction of his dreams, and endeavors to live the life which he has imagined, he will meet with a success unexpected in common hours.

—HENRY DAVID THOREAU

SECTION III

The Promised Land

In the desert, we rediscover the value of what is essential for living; thus, in today's world, there are innumerable signs, often expressed implicitly or negatively, of the thirst for God, for the ultimate meaning of life. And in the desert, people of faith are needed who, by the example of their own lives, point out the way to the Promised Land and keep hope alive.

—POPE BENEDICT XVI

CHAPTER 15

Beauty of Becoming

"Trust the wait. Embrace the uncertainty. Enjoy the beauty of becoming. When nothing is certain, anything is possible."

—MANDY HALE

I thrived in my tribes, and my unique self was taking shape through my prayers. The rescue season turned into a wilderness one. I eventually bloomed where planted. It seems this process continually repeats: uprooted, planted, blooming, and repeat. My daughter's love kept me grounded and grooving. Her notes spoke my love language to the core: "Dear Mommy, you are the best. You are a great Mommy. Love Jessica." But they could not keep me in the land of joy.

A review of my financial situation urged me to seek help again. I went to public housing, but they were not accepting applications.

What do we do? I am tired. Please, no more, no more, no more. I try to live in your name, try to be a witness, try to encourage others; my heart is yours; my life is yours, and I love you with all of me. I desire to please you. Father, why? I do not understand. How much longer? What do you want? What do I do? I am alone. I try to live holy. Oh—please, please—are you angry with me? Am I unbearable to you? So horrible

I must keep staying in the fire? I awake in the Ams with my spirit cry-
ing, "Abba Father, have mercy!" Where do you want me? Here? Where?
Please show me. Is there something else I am doing wrong? Something I
need to change? Please, mercy, mercy, mercy, mercy, mercy, grace, grace,
compassion, understanding, tenderness, solution, guidance, answers,
clear direction. Daddy, Daddy, you are my everything. Please be with
me. Show me what I can DO if anything.

God continued to respond to my heart's prayers from everywhere imaginable. I loved it, even if it was not an immediate solution or relief. Just knowing I was heard counted for much.

Once again, David Wilkerson's Times Square Church Pulpit Series had a message for me. This one was entitled, You Don't Have to Die in Your Wilderness. I chuckled when I read the title. I was still standing. I didn't die in my wilderness and truly believed I was headed into my promised land, just like the Israelites. "They may have wavered in their trial, ready to faint. But through it all, they kept their faith. How? They allowed their sufferings to drive them to their knees. As a result, their confidence in the Lord only increased. They came out of their wilderness with a testimony of God's goodness and power to deliver." This was true for me and for many who suffer trials. Remember, we decide, bitter or better. "When thou passest through the waters, I will be with thee; and through the rivers, they shall not overflow thee; when thou walkest through the fire, thou shalt not be burned; neither shall the flame kindle upon thee" (Isaiah 43:2). "For I the Lord thy God will hold the right hand, saying unto thee, Fear not; I will help thee" (Isaiah 41:13).

Mr. Wilkerson went on to share, "We see yet another testing when Israel was on the brink of the Promised Land. Twelve men were sent to spy out the land. But ten of them came back with an 'evil report.' They claimed Israel would never be able to take the land because it was filled with giants, fortresses, great walled cities, obstacles too daunting to overcome." God had loved them faithfully, just as He loved me faithfully. Yet, obstacles derailed the Israelites from entering the promised land, the land promised to them by God. Did I believe, accept, and trust in the love of my heavenly Father? Then what is there to fear? Mr. Wilkerson had a good point, "My loving Father won't allow anything to happen in my life except those things he has determined beforehand are best for me and my loved ones. No matter what my problems may be, he's going to unravel them and make a way for me. The God of Love can perform miracle after miracle on my behalf if I will only trust him." I couldn't believe what I was reading. These newsletters did this almost every time I received one. They responded to whatever current situation I was experiencing. It was surreal. This is how God works. I was reminded how God turns our ashes into beauty, or as I like to say it, our junk to jewels! God loves me and delights in me. "Therefore, we mustn't look at our obstacles. We have to keep our eyes on our Lord's great love for us." Psalm 18:17-19 tells us despite our strong enemy being too strong for us, the Lord is our stay. He will bring us forth into a large place and deliver us because he delights in us.

God is a God of grace and second chances. The beauty of the Lord is in all we are and do with His elegance, excellence, and effectiveness. I had been feeling run down and weary from the hectic schedule and daily worries, so I spent more time with God, praising, praying, and reading His Word. Single parents have many "have-tos" which cause them to just want to flee and change circumstances. I remember our Pastor speaking on this as he talked about living a significant life. He encouraged us to change the "have-tos" to "want-tos" and be willing to be made willing. Cast all your anxiety on God (1 Peter 5:7 NIV). "Cast" means to drop it. The anxiety is too heavy. Being "in bloom" illustrates a heart being willing to be made willing as God handles all the care.

JEWELS

My prayer for you right now is to not fall into "the paralysis of analysis" as I did and honestly still do occasionally. My insecurity and fear would cause me to overthink and over plan to control and prevent problems. Again, Joyce Meyer pegs what the enemy tries to do in our lives. "We allow ourselves to become overly concerned about our weaknesses. When faced with a new situation or opportunity, we often think of all the reasons why we can't do it." "God is not looking for *ability;* He's looking for our *availability.*" Our flawed thinking can get in the way.

The beauty of becoming involves spiritual warfare. Taking charge of your thoughts is key. "We demolish arguments and every pretension that sets itself up against the knowledge of God, and we take captive every thought to make it obedient to Christ" (2 Corinthians 10:5 NIV). Speaking God's Word over your life is power in your tongue. You can do anything you set out to accomplish. "I can do all this through Him who gives me strength" (Philippians 4:13 NIV).

Your words and thoughts matter. "Finally, brothers and sisters, whatever is true, whatever is noble, whatever is right, whatever is pure, whatever is lovely, whatever is admirable—if anything is excellent or praiseworthy—think about such things" (Philippians 4:8 NIV). Allow me to caution you on the act of venting. It has been believed that venting helps to get things out. Perhaps. But in this instance, your words and thoughts have a profound effect. Hugh Prather stated, "When I allow my words to reflect my negative mood, the negativity becomes more deeply rooted and powerful, and I stir up the other person as well. Now, the problem takes on a life of its own and is out of my control." Hugh gives us a pause to the art of venting, doesn't he?

The beauty of becoming incorporates how your heart loves and serves. Hugh Prather (*Love and Courage*) offers the following:

"Learning to accept yourself is the beginning of change. Learning to accept others is the beginning of wholeness. Love expands. It not only sees more and enfolds more, it causes its object to bloom."

Refuse to be average. Let your heart soar as high as it will.

—A.W. TOZER

CHAPTER 16

Promised One

"I learned that just because God loves us so much, often he guides us by planting his own lovely dream in the barren soil of a human heart. When the dream has matured, and the time for its fulfillment is ripe, to our astonishment and delight, we find that God's will has become our will and our will God's. Only God could have thought of a plan like that!"

—CATHERINE MARSHALL

There was no putting life on hold until romance happened for me. Happiness was in daily life amid hardships and heavy burdens. Looking back, I am amazed at how I did it all. None of it was possible without God orchestrating all the details and, at times, carrying me and, at other moments, supporting me. There was a never-ending juggling of responsibilities, obligations, jobs, social occasions, networking, and being a mom.

God knows exactly when my heart reached the true surrender moment, even if I did not see it in myself or the choices I made. Prayers for my second chance romance never stopped, and God sent me information and insights throughout my single mom journey. But one prayer session was significant.

Well, Lord, your will be done. I know you have your perfect plan for me to do your will; that's what I want, nothing less. If you have plans for me as a single, praise God. It will be awesome. If you have plans for me as a married woman, praise God. It will be good. However I may serve you best. My heart desires to please you. My heart as a woman also desires to have a mate, a soul mate, a man to share our love for you with each other and others, and to serve you together. A man who will love me like Jesus loved the church and a man who will cherish me. A man I may respect and honor and a man who will be my best friend, after you, Lord, and a man who loves you with all his heart, who has given himself to you first. I think you do have this for me, for Jessie and me. She desires that family. We do get lonely sometimes, Father. We will wait on you and trust in you. Thank you for each day. I give these desires to you, Lord. In your perfect timing, your plan comes together. I praise you, Father.

Lord, what are your plans for me? Make it plain. Show me. Do you want me as a single for you or do you have someone for me? Show me. Or am I to be single for a time? I will wait for an answer. I ask in Jesus' name. I love you.

A change had occurred. I knew I meant it. Serving him alone or with someone would be fine for me either way. Of course, my heart still hoped for a romantic story!

Interactions with many people continued through my insurance career, working at the restaurant, church family activities, community engagement at networking events, and membership in the Soroptimist International of St. Lucie. The second beautiful long-stemmed arrangement of flowers arrived for me from Steve, one of my new friends from the restaurant. I loved them—God knew that. They always brought a smile and made me happy.

Just a few days later, while I was sitting on our porch reading a newly purchased book, *A Man Called Peter, The Story of Peter Marshall,* written by his wife, Catherine Marshall, suddenly, I was crying as the words on the page registered meaning, "…was it possible that we together would be a greater asset to the kingdom of God than we could ever be separately?"

I went into my bedroom, got on my knees by the bed and cried, praising my Father God. I felt led to look up at my dresser. I saw my couple collection, musical globes, romance, love, man and woman, and the swan figurine (who mates for life). I smiled for I knew what God wished for me to understand. He's the one who created me and who placed my dreams and desires within my heart to begin with. Of course, I would serve Him with someone and experience romance again. I am ready! My heart was truly at peace, truly open. I died to flesh, gave my life to God, crying, "Here I am!" and meaning it. Now, God was giving me a new life. Everything is in His timing. How beautiful. I can't wait to see His plans unfold.

It is only with the heart that one can see rightly; what is essential is invisible to the eye.

—ANTOINE DE SAINT-EXUMPERY

Jessie and I walked through the aisles of Barnes & Noble, sipping our drinks and dreaming through the pages of Architectural Digest and Veranda. Such beauty! My daughter couldn't wait for our little family to grow. She shared that she would like to have a baby sister, and now she was saying, "or baby brother." Either one would make her happy.

From the moment of brokenness and despair in the land of sorrow to the emerging beauty and delight within my heart and life, an abundant number of prayers were said. And just like my creator knew the number of hairs on my head and remembered every tear shed and why, He also remembered every single prayer. These prayers were critical seeds sown as

God intertwined them into His plans for my life. Every prayer mattered. Thank goodness I had started praying from the beginning—through all the happy and sad moments—to this present day. I was co-creating with God as it pertained to my personal life and the lives of others. Words have the power to create.

My prayers helped me navigate the scary waves of life I was learning to surf. They made way for current life circumstances, with all the uncertainties combined with heart hopes, to intermingle with all God Himself desires for each of His children. As each new person made their way into my life, God used my journaling and prayers to help me understand His will and discover truths that guided important determinations, especially when it came to knowing the reason for each new male friendship.

I did not date in abundance or consistently throughout my whole singlehood, but I can tell you with absolute certainty that my desire to meet a new man who would love and cherish me never left me. I was the squeaky wheel, believe me, but I am so glad God does not always give us what we want when we want it. He knew the healing that needed to occur and how it would be accomplished. God knows when our hearts are ready. He knew what touches I needed as He molded and shaped me, and He knows what you need. For me, it was through people. Each person was used directly in my healing and self-development, and this included potential romantic partners.

God created me to be a romantic sap, and I happily own up to that. I am a Hallmark girl who loves happy endings and to see them for others. It was fun wondering if a specific person would end up becoming the "one" selected for me by God, but there was even more joy in the daily prayers and conversations I had with God about each opportunity. Romantic crushes brought hope and some happiness, but they brought disappointment, too. There were four neighbors who may have had a crush on me, and I am better for it because these men were all decent, kind, hard-working guys who treated my daughter and me very well. Their friendship and conversations were tremendously valued. In gratitude and fondness, I will always remember my three TNT Gym Mark friends who became my brother figures. I met one of them through the personal ads originally, and it was a fun day when I ran into him at my new gym! His voice got my attention right away because it was deep and husky, and in-person, he was tall and muscular—my type exactly! I had a crush on him from day one. Loved his laugh, and he reminded me of my dad, who was also a business owner and a risk-taker who knew how to get a job done.

I was an extremely insecure woman who did not have dating experience before marrying at such a young age. I did not believe myself to be attractive or pretty for a long time. After my divorce, every conversation with males seemed to bring more healing, and my confidence slowly developed along with my self-esteem. Value and worth were jewels that rose from the junk, and these relationships were key to the process.

My Polish friend Gregory, who I met as a teenager in a church youth group, ended up running into me a few times after my family moved on from that church. He liked me and asked me to be his girlfriend while we were involved in this group, but I was too insecure and afraid to say yes (a regret back then). One memory brings a smile as I write this. In high school, it was a tradition to have people turn your new high school rings the number of times of the year you were graduating. The last person was supposed to kiss you. I did not have a boyfriend at the time. I was at a Christian Petra concert, and I ran into Gregory. I don't know where my courage came from, but I just straight out asked him if he would be the one to do the final turn, and he said, "Yes!" Years later, here in Florida, I ran into a previous church member who was friends with the family, and I asked about them. She gave me his mother's phone number, and I called her. We had a beautiful conversation catching up, and from then on,

Greg and I became pen pals. His letters were arriving at perfect times, and his encouraging words had such an impact on my life. This was another of God's glorious divine appointments that continued for years. Sharing hearts with another is a vulnerable act, and it was through this sharing I gained perspective of who I was through the words of another. There was a time when I asked God if Greg was "the one" and thought how cool and creative that would be because we were getting to know each other in a safe way. But he was not my "one." I learned when he phoned me that he was getting married. I was super pleased for him and knew my day would come in God's perfect timing.

Greg was not my first pen pal. God richly blessed my heart with several pen pals who became good friends of mine: Rose DePino, Yvonne Brennan-Butler, and Allen Smith. My cousin Tina Faccento-Bense and I also wrote letters back and forth to each other. My sister, Charlene, would take time to write back to my letters even though she much preferred speaking on the telephone. These precious people valued me as a friend and encouraged me in my life while speaking the truth about my potential and worth. Their letters were a gift and a lifeline. My heart was raw with rejection, but each letter brought brighter thoughts and filled my heart. The letters have grown in their significance as God recently used them to remind me of how important it is to keep strong connections with others who see and know you, to help balance out life when certain other relationships may not be where one would have hoped them to be. Sometimes, my focus shifted to problems, and I lost sight of my significance in the whole grand scheme of things.

I went all-in on crushes—even unhealthy ones. My Hallmark girl self would dream about the possibilities (only I could see). Over time, I realized my bad patterns and many more connections revealed character traits or personality types that were not for me. Meeting the wrong types really helped me to learn what the right type looked like for me. My crush types improved as I improved. I started to crush on men who were not only handsome but healthy and productive.

JEWELS

And to be honest, while some experts have a solid, good motive for suggesting newly single parents refrain from dating for as long as possible, this was not the case for me. It was through these various interactions that I learned what was possible for me and what I should and should not allow in my life. But taking time to heal and spending quality time with your children should be your first priority. Dating may provide distraction with enjoyable moments, but it can also add more pain, confusion, or difficulties—something you or your children do not need. Plus, not dating during your most fragile timeframe prevents you from meeting potentially dangerous folks who sense your vulnerability and take advantage.

For the sake of your children and for yourself, take time to do some research and heart-searching before stepping into dating. "Rejection has a nasty way of making the healthy people we're hoping to attract hightail it like a scared rabbit the opposite direction" (Beth Moore). It will be worth your while.

Spend time healing and allow relationships into your life as they come naturally. Most times, these will be orchestrated by God to bring something to you. Remember, God's greatest desire for you is for your heart to become whole and for you to know your true value and how cherished you are. Nowadays, pen pals may not be commonplace, but reflect on your current friendships and set forth intentions to develop the ones worth developing. Make time for coffee dates with girlfriends. Romantic relationships are not the only ways you can feel beautiful. Friends bring the joy and honesty we need. Be that kind of friend to another by truly listening and being present when you're needed. Send encouraging notes and text messages. Words of the heart to another are a priceless gift that keeps on giving long after the moment it was initially received. It is hard to remain open-hearted during a season of rejection but trust me: real heart-to-heart relationships help you to know yourself and allow for appreciation and love to come your way. Amy Voskamp wrote, "It doesn't matter how your road turns, but it matters who you turn and attach to. This is all I know: Presence heals pain. Witness binds up wounds. Bonding eases trauma." Let healthy hearts get to know you. You are worth it!

Readers, you want "Heaven on Earth" in a marriage. The man must be developed in Godly fruits, patience, longsuffering, kindness, compassion, love, gentleness, mercy, self-control, and discipline. A man who has Godly wisdom, understanding, and knowledge, who will see you through eyes of Jesus, who will help you be the best you can be for Jesus and for him and your family. A man emotionally, spiritually, and physically available for you, grounded in His Jesus.

True love is friendship set on fire.

—PROVERB (AMERICAN)

CHAPTER 17
Prearranged Marriage

"The Lord bless you, my daughter!" Boaz exclaimed. "You are showing even more family loyalty now than you did before, for you have not gone after a younger man, whether rich or poor. Now don't worry about a thing, my daughter. I will do what is necessary, for everyone in town knows you are a virtuous woman."

—RUTH 3:10-11 (NLT)

Daddy, my heart is sore. Oh Father, I do so desire a relationship with a Godly man. Just the thought, how wonderful, to listen to a man speak about you, share his feelings about you, to have your tender heart, to talk about the Bible with me, a friendship to blossom—yes, even romance. To be accepted as I am. For a man to see my heart and to like what's there and to desire the inner, plus as an extra to be attracted to me physically. Daddy, I do ask, in Jesus' precious name, may I be blessed with a man sent to me from you? How special this would be.

—September 6, 2000, 8:13 p.m. Journal Entry

On and off, I would go through a period of feeling haggard, unattractive, and big. I wanted to be smaller. I felt if I were, everything would be better. One Friday morning in October of 2000, I woke up ready to make

155

some changes. I had decided it was time for me to get back into a gym. I was not at my best and needed to get there to feel better about myself. I went to a new gym and met a personal trainer, which we shall refer to as Mr. PT.

I discovered he was a Christian, and it was clear he thought I was attractive, which delighted me. He came to Lucio's to visit, and we both looked forward to getting to know each other. My coworker David thought I could do better, but I believed God answered my prayer with a new friend who made me feel pretty. Plus, I would get help, encouragement, and motivation to get in shape.

Mr. PT came over a few times and even took Jessica and me out to eat on several occasions. He seemed very nice, but there were mixed feelings from the onset. He seemed to care about things I cared about—marriage, family, certain priorities, and goals—but I had hesitations. He needed to love God first. God had someone just for me. Was it Mr. PT? Only God and time would tell.

I lost a lot of sleep during this new friendship, wondering if Mr. PT was the man God had for me and Jessie. He did have a kind heart, and my friend Lisa knew him and picked up on his kind spirit. He had nice eyes. Something about him touched me. He let me know he was thinking of me, and I liked being thought of so nicely.

He wasn't like anyone I had ever been interested in. I was trying to be open to looking beyond what my brain had always been used to and to follow my heart. I liked being with him and felt comfortable. I liked our conversations, and he seemed to have a relationship with Jesus, but I wasn't sure what kind of relationship yet. Jessica had liked him from the beginning. She told me she feels comfortable with him and could cry with him—that was comfortableness for her.

It was nice to have someone to hold hands and cuddle with, but I did not "feel" that God had sent Mr. PT to me as a husband. I didn't trust my own judgment yet, though, and wished to make sure I was making the right choice. I did discern that Mr. PT's relationship with God was not as deep or strong as mine, which bothered me.

Mutually, we decided our relationship would remain a friendship. Mr. PT was an answer to specific prayers. He helped me believe that I was beautiful, on the inside for sure, and yes, even on the outside. He had confirmed that God had done a wonderful, life-changing transformation and that I would be God's gift to a husband. A blessing. A wife that would be cherished and desired by a man of God's choosing.

We remained friends, and once he stopped in for dinner during my shift and came over afterward. We talked and cuddled, and I thought maybe there would be more to our friendship after all. I had been afraid of going too fast, and shared my feelings, to which he agreed. Many nights later, Mr. PT came over after his workout and stayed late. That's when I decided to put a stop to things and stop putting myself in situations I was not ready for.

I prayed that night and asked God to forgive me, for my thoughts and actions. My body, heart, and soul desired to be loved and held and to make love with a man. Mr. PT's touches made me yearn for more, but I also wanted things the way God would do them. I wanted a relationship with someone that God sent. I desired to be sought after, romanced, for it to progress in a good, clean, Godly way. I was upset, kind of peeved, and sad—maybe a little of everything. I thought it was unfair at times. I desired God's utmost and wanted to please him. But walking in purity then (and in this day and age) was hard.

Yes, I desired to have Mr. PT make love to me, but it would not have been right. It was not the time. I desired to have a union with a man on my wedding night.

Another Tuesday night Bible study had rolled around, and the ladies prayed for me. I still sensed Mr. PT was not the man God had for me, but I was in his life to encourage him. We had let our humanness, earthly desires, needs, and weaknesses take us on a side trip.

Work at the restaurant was brutal one evening; busy, short-staffed, and I had fallen hard on my knee and hurt my ankle and back in the process as well. After church the next morning, Jessie and I enjoyed breakfast at our special place, Café Crème. She and I relaxed at home until we picked up Mr. PT and went to the Teddy Bear concert we previously committed to. The music was beautiful, and afterwards Mr. PT treated us to Wendy's and even bought Jessie a cute Teddy bear. But I felt disappointed he was not where I was in my walk with God. I was sold out. He was not.

We would have to remain just friends. I was still a slow thinker and even slower at making final decisions due to fear of making the wrong choice. I would finally come to recognize the pattern, but it still took me even more time to process everything and formulate my plan of action. Thankfully, ultimately, because I had God as my priority, all roads and decisions led me in His direction with the right decision.

My coworker from the restaurant, David, asked to speak with me privately. Outside, he told me he had to appraise me, he thought that it was great that Mr. PT and I chilled it because we wanted different things. He respected that I had standards and stuck to them. It was nice to hear from someone who had often given me a hard a time. God had a godly man for me; I just had to wait. As hard as it got sometimes, or lonely, nothing compared to being pleasing to God.

I was withdrawn at Lucio's later that evening. Everyone I worked with had noticed, and at the end of the night, we all ended up chatting. When they asked why I was no longer seeing Mr. PT, I explained that he couldn't be in a relationship without sex. They all had opinions, but John strongly suggested I be more specific with my prayers on what kind of man I desired for a husband. So, in front of all of Lucio's, I started my list.

In Jesus' name, here are some of the qualities I desire in a husband.

- His heart—he loves you with his whole heart.

- He loves you first and has a strong relationship with you.

- He is sensitive to your spirit.

- He hears from you daily.

- Heart for ministry—serving you, kids.

- Taller than me.

- Big, solid, a little muscular.

- Attractive to me—he takes my breath away, the way he talks, his smile, eyes, voice.

- He loves beautiful music, art, plays, and operas.

- He loves to travel.

- To experience new things.

- To enjoy beautiful places, things, and flowers, like them, like to buy them.

- He wears nice cologne.

- Handsome in his clothes.

- Educated.

- Financially stable, secure, and well-off would be a super blessing.

- Loves to read.

- Loves to go to the beach.

- Loves to talk about everything.

- A touchy person always wants to hold hands or have his arm around you.

- Father, he has your heart, the fruits of your spirit; the other stuff is an added blessing.

Around that same time, my neighbor Mike and I started talking. He also lived in our building, and his vehicle parking spot was right next to mine. Sometimes, we spoke on the telephone during the evenings, and he found me attractive. Mike was a nice man but had no relationship with God, so I knew I couldn't consider our relationship anything other than a friendship.

The days went by.

Frustrations in my career as an insurance agent also continued.

I remember having an interesting day at the office when I met with a marketing rep, a nice man named Chris Cooper, from the marine industry for the first time.

A week or so later, I had a fabulous, divine-appointment-kind-of-day when Chris and I met for coffee. It turned out he was a Christian and married. Since I was trying to find my niche and a market in which I could easily place new business, I was pleased to have this opportunity to learn more about this industry. But more importantly he had given me a CD that had been produced at his MCRS Studios in 1999 entitled JC John & Chris "Keep it Simple."

Later that afternoon at home, with much anticipation, I listened to it while worshipping and praising God. I found myself face down on the floor. In prayer, I gave God my desires and my tiredness. I cried and poured out my heart. The lyrics and melodies soothed my spirit. I had such a special time with Daddy God. I felt his tender, loving touch—his presence—where I so wanted to stay, but I couldn't because I had to pick up Jessie from school. I had such a quiet peace. Chris Cooper's work was anointed and perfectly spoke to my heart. What Chris may have thought of as a simple gesture of sharing his music was simply and profoundly Heaven-sent. God knew exactly what my weary heart needed.

More healing came on one of our mommy-daughter days when Jessie shared that she loved our home! We were blessed with God, with each other, and yes, we had a beautiful, godly, peaceful home. After sleeping in (what a luxury) and a leisurely breakfast, we ended up at Morningside Library. The two of us enjoyed ourselves tremendously, taking our time browsing through all the books. It was mutually agreed upon to add the library to our things we do together list.

* * *

Waiting on God to fulfill His promises can be difficult and discouraging. I got weary in the waiting. I remember crying one day and telling God we needed an emergency session. I lay on the floor face down with my Bible and prayed. My heart guided my prayers as circumstances dictated the requests, and they mingled together. Prayers uttered forth, and I heard myself asking for a prearranged marriage like God did for Isaac and Rebekah. This arrangement worked for them, and I trusted God to do as well for my daughter and me.

God must have liked my idea because it wasn't that long after, on June 11, 2001, during my regular morning Bible reading, that a scripture jumped out at me. This occurs when the Holy Spirit brings to our attention an application for a current situation or need for direction. God had spoken to me through His Word like this on other occasions, and the timing was divine.

Ruth 3:10-11 (NKJV) spoke to me: "...Blessed are you of the Lord, my daughter. For you have shown more kindness at the end than at the beginning, in that you did not go after young men, whether poor or rich. And now, my daughter, do not fear. I will do for you all that you request, for all the people of my town know that you are a virtuous woman." I couldn't believe it! Not that God uses His Word to speak to us, but on how precise His scripture was in response to my specific ask. Now I knew God not only had someone special for me, but He would personally select Him out for my daughter and me, like He did with Boaz for Ruth and her mother-in-law.

JEWELS

My training and development were nonstop. God continued to prepare me for the future, including detailed examples of good, godly men. And yes, another David Wilkerson's Times Square Church Pulpit Series newsletter, his "These Men have been with Jesus" issue, which I read on October 5, 2001, was used.

> *"Likewise, I believe this will be God's powerful witness in these last days. It won't come through preaching alone. It will come also through men and women who "have been with Jesus": shutting themselves in with him, spending time in his presence, seeking him with all their heart and soul. The Holy Spirit will distinguish such servants with his power. And the world will say of them, "That person has been with Christ."*

Here are four distinguishing marks of those who have been with Jesus:

1. They hunger for a greater measure of Christ.

2. They have a holy boldness and spiritual authority.

3. They have physical, visible evidence that God is with them.

4. They're prepared for any crisis.

"What greater evidence of God could there be, than a single life transformed by the supernatural power of Christ? May it be said of you, 'That man, that woman, has been with Jesus.' And may no one be able to deny it."

This is a man I desired to meet someday. And I was sure this man would respect my values, would hear me when I spoke, and would add to who I was as a person. The struggle to try and live my life modeled after what the Bible spoke about would be worth it. My "wait" was not a perfect one, but I strived to be all God desired me to be with His help, to hold out for God's best for me as best as I could. Wait for God's best for you.

You are worth being in a relationship with someone who values and cherishes you as the treasure God created you to be. There is a massive difference between a man who strives to please God and has faith compared to one who does not. It matters and shows up in all the little life details and large life circumstances. Who do you desire to have as a mate, as a life partner? Take time to think about this and pray about this. Maybe you will wish to create a list like I did, and the list above can help you. This is the type of man worth waiting for. A man with a heart for God. You and your children deserve this. Discernment does take time, and maybe, like me, your emotional health is undergoing a healing journey, and you may not recognize obvious signs, and maybe you are a slow processer too. Keep good friends around you and solicit plenty of feedback from those you love and trust.

In all proper relationships, there is no
sacrifice of anyone to anyone.

—ANY RAND

CHAPTER 18

Fallen – Not Forsaken

"And Jabez called on the God of Israel saying, "Oh, that You would bless me indeed, and enlarge my [a]territory, that Your hand would be with me, and that You would keep me from evil, that I may not cause pain!" So God granted him what he requested."

—THE JABEZ PRAYER, 1 CHRONICLES 4:10 (NKJV)

It has been said that before any major miracle, there is massive hardship. In my experience, things get worse before they get better. I fell and fell hard.

I messed up and fell off my abstinence before the marriage trek. The date and the deed will forever be remembered. It's in my Bible, and I wrote an essay about the experience for my psychology class (which earned an "A," by the way), so there is some redemption. I am certainly not perfect. Yes, I did try to be a good girl in all the ways I thought that meant. Remember, I was a virgin before getting married (but had no idea about making sure it was the right man, right time). I was a rule follower (mostly) and tried to live a righteous life as the Bible describes. I had slipped only once before during my single mom years after too much champagne. That relationship did not continue.

That mess-up left me devastated. Receiving affirmations to this point in my life primarily came from being a "good" girl, receiving good grades, being responsible, and doing the right thing. I ran to Jesus, repented, received forgiveness, and rededicated myself to living a life that would be pleasing to God but also as a good example for my daughter. Abstinence was absolutely working for me—until it didn't.

A prospective client I had kept in touch with for over a year had finally agreed to see me to discuss his insurance program. We agreed that I would come by his office at the end of the day. I was looking forward to it, intrigued by this man whom I had several conversations with. Let's call him Mr. Surveyor.

I was wearing my elegant, classy pink and white dress suit. Our meeting was going well. He was handsome and finely dressed, which I always appreciated in a man. His scent was enticingly sensual. Good cologne was my undoing. During our meeting, he showed off pictures of his kids, and I liked his accent.

The scheduling of this appointment was remarkable, as I had just resigned to start school full time to earn my AA degree. The commission from selling a few more policies before I left the agency would be a blessing. He decided he would allow me to quote on his business liability.

"I can give you the information you need to get started over dinner," he calmly said.

Excuse me? My heart raced. He'd just asked me to dinner. He seemed so sophisticated, and I was nervous all over again. At first, I politely declined. Isn't that what all good-mannered girls do? I couldn't let my brand-new potential client take me out to dinner. Or could I? Wasn't I supposed to be the one taking him out? Wasn't that how business deals went?

He persisted. He was famished. The day had been overwhelmingly hectic, and he hadn't eaten since breakfast. The restaurant was right down the street.

He was quite bold. I ended up accepting his offer, as Jessie was with her father that night.

At the restaurant, I was afraid to order an actual dinner item. I couldn't believe the prices, but dinner was delicious, and the décor was fabulous. I felt so pampered. I couldn't believe I was sitting in this restaurant eating with this man. The conversation was good, and he was fascinating. Of course, I had wine with my dinner, and the liquid flowed throughout the evening. I loved how he made me feel so pretty.

After dinner, we walked out to our cars. He asked if he could come over.

I was shocked and declined.

He asked again.

I declined again.

He persisted.

Later, I would realize this was typical behavior.

I said I don't do that.

Do what?

I don't have guys come back to my place.

Why not?

I am a Christian. No sex. I was blunt. It must have been the wine.

He laughed! Is that what you think?

Yes, that is exactly what I think.

I just want to keep talking with you.

I had never been in this situation before. No, usually meant no. But I liked talking to him. If he came over, what would happen? Was he really going to drive all the way to my place to then go home? That was quite a drive. I said as much to him.

No big deal, he assured me.

As I got in my car, he said he would just follow me and started toward his car. I wanted to scream or cry or probably do both. Now what? What do I say? What did I want to do? What should I do? I tried again to tell him no.

"Listen, I must get up early the next morning. Thank you for a wonderful dinner, and I appreciate you seeing me to discuss your insurance needs. I look forward to working on your quotes and will call you during the week. I hope you have a good night."

He walked back over and stood right next to me. I mean right next to me. In my space. I could smell his cologne, and my insides became mush. No, he couldn't come over that would not be good. But even now, he was insisting he just wanted to spend more time with me and continue our conversation. He didn't want to go home yet. His kids were with their mom. Well, that I could understand. How many times did I just wish for someone to be near for me to talk with? Maybe he was sincere. I relented. He hugged me, smiled, and quickly walked away back toward his car. I was beside myself.

A man was coming to my apartment. A professional man who owned his own business and had children was coming to my place. As I was driving home, the smile was there. Fear was there, too. What the hell was I doing? Wasn't I putting myself in a difficult position? What if he wasn't sincere? But I didn't want to be alone either. I couldn't believe a man was following me home. I was excited, scared, nervous, curious, and flattered. Was this happening?

Yes, it was. We arrived at my apartment complex, and I was giggling.

He sensed my nervousness and started laughing, too. He thought it was cute, and I was so nervous. He liked where I lived.

I started to tell him all about our place, about the pool, and the nice neighbors as we went up the stairs. Inside, I gave him the official tour and could sense him right behind me the whole time, that delicious scent everywhere. It had been too long.

He was impressed with my apartment and followed me back to the living room. I felt his breath on my neck, and when I turned around, he kissed me. My senses were overloaded. He had his hands on my face as we kissed, and I couldn't think. He was moving me. Where? I had no idea. We were on the floor now. He removed my white pumps and pulled down my white tights. No one had done that before. The kissing was getting deeper and stronger. His tongue was doing a dance, and I was somewhere I don't ever remember being, not even in my ten and a half years of marriage to my ex-husband. I'd never been kissed like this. Now, he was on top of me. I felt like I was having an out-of-body experience; parts of me felt what was happening, but the other parts were not in sync. This shouldn't be happening, but the dormant parts of me were revolting and not listening to reason. Here I was, messing up, sinning big time but could not even enjoy the experience. What is wrong with me? What fun is sin if you are not having fun? Why sin if you feel too guilty to enjoy it? The need to be touched, held, and kissed was beyond my ability to stop. It had been a long time. Heck, I was living in the desert! I did enjoy the kissing. Being desired by him made me feel wanted. He left soon after. There was no conversation as mentioned would be, only the tour, quite the tour.

One of my deepest heartfelt prayers to my Father was that He "keep" me until I met and married my next husband. With all my heart, I want to live my life to please God. Having sex outside of marriage is not something I wanted. Yes, there have been many hard days and nights where I did cry out to God to help me, to have mercy, to quickly send that man to marry me, to marry me before I messed up, not to have me mess up. I had thanked Him for protecting me from so many circumstances.

So, why did a door that was slammed shut open? Why, after all those years, did I lose control? I met someone nice, which has happened before. We went to dinner, which has happened before. He came over afterward, and we started to fool around, which has happened before. But then we were doing things which *hadn't* happened before. On one hand, I knew what I was doing, but I also knew I didn't *want* to be doing it—but I didn't stop it. My heart was not involved; it wasn't how it was supposed to be. Making love should be between two people who *love* each other and have *already* committed their hearts to each other and who are in a marriage. It is not meant to be any other way. Oh, how I cried right after he left, a deep cry.

I do not know what happened exactly. I experienced many thoughts and emotions, some of which I captured in my journal to God when I was ready to do so.

09/01/01: Father, what has happened? Please advise. Please show me. I have fallen. Will you pick me up? My heart is yours—was yours. What happened? I pray to keep me from evil. What happened? I pray keep me, help me, to please you. I prayed for compassion and mercy and to keep us strong. What have I done, God? I cried out to you many times, "DO NOT LET ME EVER DO IT WRONG." I desired with everything that is within me to obey your word, to do things your way, your timing, waiting on you, daily asking for your strength, to be a woman of faith, godliness, and holiness—effective for you in every way. Now what? Where do I go from here? It's so sad, so futile. I walk a certain way for so long. You have kept me for so long. Then all of a sudden BAM, done, over, all gone. Everything I had waited for from you, is it gone forever? Father, I am sorry. Words cannot describe how I feel. I let you down. I let myself down. I am VERY disappointed with myself. I know what your word says. What did I do? Why? For whom? I am confused. Am I not your kid, your daughter? You are our cover. What has happened and why? Why Father? Why now? Why? WHY? Forgive me. Where is the man you have for me? Surely, this is not what you had in mind. Is it Father? Show me, please, clearly. You have directed all my steps. YOU are in charge. I do not understand. Help me do what needs to be done. I was not strong enough, bold enough. How could I

NOT stand? Father, why could I NOT stand? Please, did I hurt you? How is your heart? Mine is hurt, disappointed, confused. Will you just let me go now? Is it over between us? I was hoping on, counting on, coming out of my wilderness on your arms, leaning on you—coming out victorious, stronger in faith, but no, now look. Father, did I do this? How could I do this? Are you not carrying me any longer? I felt secure in your arms. Did I take advantage—Daddy, Daddy, Daddy, please hear and respond. I wait. If not you, then nothing. Absolutely nothing.

I was disgusted with myself. I had known better.

Maybe I had become too confident in my walk with God on this issue. This was one of my major testimonies of what the Lord can do. We can abstain from having sex with God's help. I was living proof. Now, I was afraid I would lose the greatest source of love I had come to know and receive from God.

My prayers uttered one thing, but reality was a different matter entirely. Mr. Surveyor was zealous in his pursuit. He called me every day. We got together on various occasions to do things together. He came to the restaurant where I worked on the weekends. He left a $20 tip each time he came, sweetness. I even met his children.

The conversations I had with God continued throughout the many months this superficial relationship continued. Prayers, tears, pleas for mercy, forgiveness, and help were whispered or shouted constantly.

I shared my heart and words with this man over and over about who I really was and what I wanted for my life. I was like the Sandhill Crane I observed from my apartment window. The bird locked eyes on another bird he saw, which was just his reflection on the car window, and proceeded to peck the other bird/car relentlessly. I didn't get it—not till much later.

With every conversation I had with Mr. Surveyor and every letter I sent, I was asking and then pleading with him to be the man my heart was yearning for. Turns out, even though I love learning and was a straight "A" student, when it comes to matters of life, I was a slow learner—crockpot slow. I wanted the real thing, and that meant enough was enough. I wanted to go all the way and feel good about it. I didn't want that out-of-body experience. Why bother? This door was not going to just shut on its own. No, I had to stand tall and realize my worth and value and slam this door myself. Another door with the real prize would never open unless I did so. So, I did.

I remember my first struggle when feeling abandoned, unloved, lonely, and vulnerable. The devil will set us up and attack where we once experienced vulnerability, what we knew from our past, our old language, what we were familiar with, and past generational ways of communicating or receiving love. There is temptation before we experience our breakthrough. I knew God had someone special for me and had special plans for my life. The enemy of our soul desires to distract us and have us settle, but God doesn't. God desires that we soar as eagles. "But those who trust in the Lord will find new strength. They will soar high on wings like eagles. They will run and not grow weary. They will walk and not faint" (Isaiah 40:31 NIV). Would I allow myself to miss out on what God has planned for me? Would I remain in the flesh, experiencing the same old ways of being loved, accepting love, taking scraps and crumbs, and accepting relationships where there was no emotional availability, which told me repeatedly I didn't matter? Would I live where generational sins, brokenness, hurt, and pain ran my life? The devil wishes to keep repeating the same old stuff and put us in emotional prisons. God desires me to be free in every way imaginable, receiving the love He desires for me, being in healthy two-way relationships where I do matter, where I am important, of worth, value, and matter greatly! To be enjoyed by someone else!

Patrick Mabilog, in his article entitled "Why Do Things Get Bad Before the Breakthrough Comes?" states, "There are two prerequisites to a great miracle: the undeniable power of the Holy Spirit through Jesus Christ and a difficult circumstance that cannot be overcome on our own. Many times, God brings us through situations that seem to go from bad to worse as His way of sifting out the trust of the self and allowing only the trust of God to take over." He goes on to say, "the same way a plane shakes intensely when it's about to hit the speed of sound, life shakes terribly when we're about to receive our miracle. This shaking is the opposition in this world that doesn't want you to receive your breakthrough. John 10:10 tells us, 'The thief comes only to steal and kill and destroy. I came that they may have life and have it abundantly' (ESV). In all we do, there is a thief—the devil—who wants you to stay stuck, and he's going to give you the fight of a lifetime. And as discouraging as it may be when those shakings and trials come, we can stand firm, knowing that the shaking comes only because the enemy is desperate; he knows he's about to lose, and he tries to do everything in his power to escape unscathed."

All my days were grace days. God was taking care of my daughter and me with divine appointments and miracles. I had believed God would leave us and stop caring for us. But guess what? God never forsook us. "I will never leave you nor forsake you" (Hebrews 13:15 NKJV). Throughout the whole season of thinking (and hoping) this man may be our "Boaz" to knowing he was not, God never left. His care never stopped. As a matter of fact, His presence increased, and He brought more people into our lives to guide us and show us what He envisioned for us.

One day, while I was in prayer and worshipping God, after I told Him how much I love Him and thanked Him for healing me and making me beautiful, He responded!

I am your little girl who loves you so, so very much. This is my love letter that I am singing to you now. I love you, Father God. You truly have filled us with your goodness. Thank you for a full life in you, for your joy and happiness. You have healed this broken, sad, insecure, empty girl. Praise you. Thank you, thank you. Your Georgette Michel loves you. Who I am "is" you, what you have created. Thank you for what your hands have done with me. I love you. Praise you for all the miracles. We will see and experience it through you! The Lord has heard my cries. He has answered from most high. Praise Him, for he is good. He hears, he knows, from His holy hills. He extends his hand to us. Our lord God reigns. Mighty, powerful, gracious is our God, tender most kind.

God responded to my spirit, "Daughter, daughter, precious are you. A jewel, fine, one of a kind, sweet, precious, opal."

The word opal is from the Sanskrit *upala*, which means "jewel," and is known as the Queen of Gemstones and considered a semi-precious stone, the stone of kings. They symbolize confidence, loyalty and represent hope, purity, happiness, and faithfulness.

Not too long after receiving this word from God, I received a card from someone in our church family filled with $100.00 cash with the message, "May this help and bless you. Your sister and family in Christ Jesus."

Of all the male friendships I was thankful to have encountered, I had always wondered why, for my massive fall, was it with the particular man it was with, a relationship that took about ten months to work through. I guess I wondered what it may have been about him that I was no longer able to remain strong in my abstinent lifestyle. He had a strong personality. He was used to getting his way. He was a businessman and a survivor too maybe from a tough childhood. He did remind me of my dad's strength and ability to achieve, but my dad differed in how he treated my mom with love and respect, not that my dad did not make mistakes, he did, but he had more value for how others were treated. My spirit knew this man was not for me, but my heart and head went back and forth like a yo-yo. I did eventually catch up to where my spirit and heart would ultimately lead me with God at the front. Good friends surrounded me, and even my crushes at this time were with healthier people. God had since revealed to me that this was one of those Heavenly mysteries. This person represented generational repeats that had occurred in my family for I don't know how many generations. And God had set in motion an end to this repeated pattern. I was now a healthier, more healed, woman who was the first in the family to become a college-educated, spirit-filled woman who loved her Jesus. God made way for restoration to occur from what the enemy of our soul had stolen and taken not just from me but from my parents, grandparents, and so forth. God had been on a mission to not only heal my heart, but He was healing all hearts in my family and busy setting forth in motion destiny restoration which would come to full realization years later. Only God knew what would have occurred within my spirit and heart from my time at Oral Roberts University, never mind what opportunities I may have realized if I had taken that destiny path. God was preparing me for what He envisioned for me. I was in a battle way over my head, but God was fighting on my behalf.

JEWELS

Always know we may fall, but God will never forsake us.

"Many of us, like Naaman, will face the uncomfortable before the miracle. The truth is that the path to a miracle often goes through uncomfortable territory that will force us to depend on God, to trust in His promises. Think of the beautiful stories in the Bible where people were led to miracles through discomfort … Israel endured years of discomfort before they could enter the Promised Land. David was doubted before he slew

Goliath. As a wedding party panicked, Jesus miraculously turned water to wine. In your season of discomfort, I call you to rejoice in it. It is simply a reminder of all the good that is soon to come. May your prayer today be, 'God, help me to see your will in my discomfort. Help me to recognize the glory of Your ways, to see that the uncomfortable comes just before a miracle'" (NGK, The Uncomfortable Before the Miracle, timetogetready.org).

Please be gentle, kind, and compassionate with yourself. Sometimes, it takes time to see the truth. Breaking free from past spiritual wounds and generational pains, sins, and deep stuff is something only God can handle. Keep your focus on Him, His Word, and the vision He has for you. Have daily heart-to-heart moments with God. Here is where you receive guidance, hope, encouragement, and help. Keep praying and journaling about your experiences, and meditate on the scriptures that speak to your situation. Eventually, you will become sick and tired of being sick and tired, and the truth will reveal itself in unquestionable ways, and you will see the way forward. Your failures are the fertile soil where wisdom is best gleaned for future impact. "Learning starts with failure, the first failure is the beginning of education" (John Hersey).

Supposing you have tried and failed again and again, you may have a fresh start any moment you choose, for this thing that we call "failure" is not the falling down, but the staying down.

—MARY PICKFORD

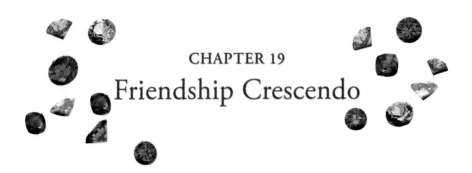

CHAPTER 19
Friendship Crescendo

"Because everything of value that we will know in this life comes from our relationships with those around us. Because there is nothing material that measures against the intangibles of love and friendship."

—R.A. SALVATORE

I was blessed to have met many acquaintances during my single season. So many friends were instrumental in helping me discover the truth about myself. My heart is full of the memories and relationships brought into my life when they were needed the most.

Our relationships mirror our spiritual and emotional condition. As I healed and developed through the years, my relationships seemed to be better aligned with me. Sometimes, my new friends would overlap at various points, especially at the end of my single mom season. I am reminded of a crescendo musical passage. This was how it was before our "Boaz" came to us. I laugh out loud with joy and amazement at this memory. God used specific positive relationships and good people all at once to bring the point home for me—and even one perceived as a negative relationship—but one ultimately to help me make the urgent destiny decision I needed to make.

Mr. Surveyor was the only relationship that turned truly romantic in the sense that there were dates, kissing, and sporadic physical intimacy, but

I knew he wasn't for me. He was the one I perceived as a negative relationship. Golly, even many of my friends and family knew he wasn't for me, but I struggled to say "no more" and mean it.

I learned that my failure was something God used to heal the generational pattern within my family. I was meant to meet this person. As God worked to pull up those generational roots, He brought in reinforcements to bring home His truth and plans for my life in a lively, almost musical manner.

* * *

A new neighbor, who I shall refer to as Mr. Mercedes, moved into our apartment building in June 2002, ten months after the whole season of my trying to walk away from Mr. Surveyor who, on this day, was still in my life.

Jessie thought Mr. Mercedes was "sweet." He was kind, but those first few interactions and conversations did not make it clear what the purpose of our meeting each other was. In time, God would reveal His purpose, and if he was the one God selected, we would all know.

Mr. Mercedes was a man of faith and seemed to have the same love of communication as I did. He would call me but also leave written notes and letters—written words were my primary language! I really enjoyed learning about him in this manner. We would talk for an hour and sometimes longer on other occasions.

He invited me to go to his church with him.

He shared with me that when he came home and did not see my car, he was disappointed.

He shared about himself, his life, and his family.

After I went to church with him, he shared how it affected him when I cried during the Sunday service. He also shared how he was praying in church about a Christian wife and felt God within answering—"she's sitting right next to you."

I personally thought differently. I thought God had blessed me with a good friendship in the making. I wasn't sure about anything more than that. The age difference between the two of us was quite a bit. He was older than my dad, and I wasn't comfortable with this.

When I went out dancing with friends one night, I made another new acquaintance: Mr. Landscaper. We conversed the rest of the evening, and he asked for my phone number before I left with our group of friends.

That same night I came home to find a heartfelt emotional letter from Mr. Mercedes, sharing his feelings of love for Jessie and me, of wanting me to marry him. I thought how nice it would be to be taken care of, for us to no longer worry, with our refrigerator bare, bills to pay, rent to come up with, camp money, uniform money, new clothes desired, hair appointment, etc. I had waited so long for the right man to come along who would declare his feelings of admiration and devotion—just like Mr. Mercedes seemed to be doing. Of course, I gave it all to my Father: the letters, words, His promises to us, our hearts, thoughts, and questions. He would work it all out in his timing. It would all just naturally flow together peacefully like all He does.

My heart realized one day that, just like Jessie was so innocently glad to see Mr. Mercedes on her return trip from Connecticut—she was jumping up and down—the spirit in me, too, was like a little girl's. I was giddy to receive his notes, always getting a little thrill when an envelope sat on our door.

I had been asking God to keep speaking to me and show me what his intentions were. What was His will? Is this the man He has selected for us? The one promised? In my flesh, I would say it can't be; the age difference and lack of physical chemistry are holding me back. Spiritual things were truly my heart's desire, but I still wanted a physical connection.

Mr. Landscaper kept in contact and even came over a few times.

One evening that I had three of my current "friends" inside my apartment visiting with me, and afterward, Mr. Mercedes told me I should choose one to be a boyfriend as they were all interested in pursuing more with me.

"Georgette," he said, "There will be no perfect person."

Each "friend" had the potential for a commitment, but ultimately, they were not the one God had for me. Yet, each of them reiterated my value and worth and profoundly impacted my ability to break free from the entanglement I was desiring to move away from to be free for the right man. I understood there would be no perfect person, but I was doing my best to hold out for the person God thought would be perfect for me!

I was not officially dating any of them, but I continued to pray and tell God my questions and doubts. With His help, I slowly reached my own conclusions.

Mr. Mercedes went to dinner with me a few times, and we had a wonderful time. He even sat down with me and helped me with my finances and a budget. I would be okay, but there was still more to do.

Monday night, Jessica and I had dinner with Mr. Surveyor's sister, who was in town at his condominium. I had become friends with her, and we wrote letters and emails to each other. Visiting her at her brother's home was a conflict of interest in my heart. I still held a desire to be with him, but I had more peace in our remaining just as friends. I felt sad. I'd developed feelings for a man I had no business being close to and who possessed traits I did not desire in my life. What could ever become of this? Nothing. Per God's Word: "Do not be unequally yoked." I still had lessons to learn.

I came home from that visit and cried quietly, praying. I realized I did love Mr. Surveyor, but I felt hurt and sad. They were sad memories, not full of peace or joy.

My heart conflicted with my head and changing took time. It would've been easy to give in and do what I'd always done, but God had healed me and provided a path. Now I had to learn to walk through it, even when hard. Journaling was powerful. I loved that journaling revealed patterns of thought and helped me to confront my unhelpful behavior.

God's will for me involved things that aligned with the Scriptures. God treated me with love, respect, tenderness, and compassion. My mate should be like that. I was harsh on myself, but I observed that my intuition knew the truth and knew exactly what I desired and deserved for me and my daughter. I should not settle, not ever. God was accomplishing the final inner work. To walk away involved much more than I understood at the time. This was a spiritual battle—to leave what was perceived as love despite not being heard or respected. It was something I had not been able to do with Damien. I was God's cherished little girl. Pain like this was not His plan for my life. He would pull up the strongholds of this flesh bond and break the chains that bound me to this circumstance. The conflict was hard—spirit versus flesh—and the battle heated up closer and closer to the date of Boaz's arrival, the man of promise from God.

* * *

Jessica and I experienced more divine happenstance when we found out about scholarships available for families wishing to send their children to a private school. God made a way for her to go back to her spiritual family and peers at Morningside Academy, and we were both thrilled. She had a fabulous first day back!

My birthday was eight days away! I would be turning 34.

Meanwhile, Mr. Landscaper had been calling to check in, and I invited him over to watch a movie. This was back in the days of Blockbuster, and Jessie and I managed to treat ourselves to new movies often. It felt good to be sitting next to each other on the couch, holding hands. He respected my desire for our friendship to progress very slowly. But even though I thought Mr. Landscaper was a nice, quality guy, I did not have romantic feelings toward him.

Jessica and I met Mr. Mercedes for dinner, and he came over afterward to play a game with Jessica and talk with me. It was nice to talk to him about personal things, and it helped me feel better being able to share with a friend. He called me on the phone that night after he left, and we talked for almost another hour. I still believed this man was placed behind Jessie and me on purpose by God because of His goodness to both of us. Our friendship was special, but Mr. Mercedes still felt more toward me than I felt toward him. He desired more than friendship. But I saw him as a brother, maybe part of a Father-daughter relationship as well. A male mentor whom I admired and enjoyed being with.

Soon thereafter, I went again to Mr. Mercedes' church. Communion was served, but before that, the pastor had a special altar call and asked anyone to come up who needed prayer to break any holds over them. Something we could not break from, to let God's spirit do it. I had to respond, knowing there was a hold over me concerning Mr. Surveyor.

I was finally able to let go of Mr. Surveyor. I truly felt Jesus had broken the power of sin over me. I was healed and set free.

As I listened to Celine Dion's "A New Day Has Come," the words rang true. Her song confirmed God's promise of a new song for my life. I also received a rhema word—a personal and timely spoken word or message from God meant to bring direction, encouragement, or correction—regarding deliverance, from Jeremiah 26:2-6.

* * *

Now, only four days to my special day, I was sad. I had grown quite attached to my friend Mr. Mercedes. Something about him drew me in, but I couldn't get past how uncomfortable our age difference made me feel.

One night before I went to work, I made a huge mistake in being too honest with him, sharing how I felt embarrassed by the age difference. I was uncomfortable with it, but it was my problem, I told him. Well, my honesty hurt him. I did care about him. I liked him so much, and I was an idiot. When I came home the following morning, a bag of books he'd borrowed, along with a note, was hanging on my door. It was a cruel, mean note. It tore my heart to shreds, hurt to the core. I cried. Some of what he said did bring me up short, and I received from it for what I should receive.

Everything he said about Mr. Surveyor was true.

That morning, I took communion with God, and it did something in me. Mr. Mercedes had forsaken me, shut me out, dissed me, cut me off. I had shared my heart, my life, and my thoughts with him; I loved him as my friend. The anguish left me empty, but I praised God through it and for it because I learned from all my mistakes. Pain did have a way of getting my attention and opening my eyes.

I could never totally enjoy myself with Mr. Mercedes due to fear of what others would say.

I was grateful for my mended relationship with my family during this period. I loved them, and we'd gotten closer. We laughed and cared about things together more. We talked a bit about what had happened with Mr. Mercedes, and Mom spoke a few good words of encouragement.

At the altar call, I'd felt I'd finally been able to let Mr. Surveyor go, but the note from Mr. Mercedes was a fresh rejection, opening old wounds.

* * *

On September 6, 2002, after not having seen Mr. Surveyor for a while, he asked if he could take me to Sakura's for dinner. Now that we were just friends, I didn't see anything wrong with going to dinner, especially for delicious sushi. He had given me a leather pocketbook—elegant and classy—from his country as a belated birthday gift. It was perfect for my new sophisticated image.

At dinner, he asked me to be his girlfriend and talked of marrying me. After I shared about wanting to pursue my dreams—complete my college education, take a trip to Europe, maybe write, speak, who knows—he offered to help me with school. He tried to sway me. I wouldn't have to work, and he would take me to Europe. I would be happy being married to him. But I could not commit or agree to anything; he didn't love or serve the Lord the way I needed. We were not one in the spirit. The evening left me sad once again. He just never got it. But I did.

JEWELS

Quality friendships are good for your health. Literally! The Mayo Clinic published an online article, "Friendships: Enrich Your Life and Improve Your Health," where they confirm that good friends are good for your health, prevent isolation and loneliness, increase your sense of belonging and purpose, boost your happiness and reduce stress, improve your self-confidence and self-worth, and help you cope with traumas and encourage you to change unhealthy lifestyle habits. I can confirm this all to be true for me, and I'm thinking for you, too.

My church family was a solid community where my daughter and I found healthy, life-transforming friendships. These people of all ages were truly there for my daughter and me—even more so than my own family—especially at the beginning of my healing journey. Later, when my own family and I experienced relationship healing, they, too, became integral to our daily lives.

The desire to meet a potential new mate was always there, but it wasn't always a good time to pursue this. Meeting males, father figures, and brother figures in the safety of a church community was conducive to much of the healing that needed to occur within me. Later, God used various male acquaintances and friendships developed through my work life and then my social life.

God used these relationships to develop my personality, self-esteem, and confidence. These relationships strengthened my ability to communicate and carry myself in a variety of situations and helped me evolve as a woman who came to understand her value. I learned that my worth is not dependent on a relationship or another person; these are inner traits you gain recognition of as you grow in your relationship with your creator, God. But I must say, God loves to use everything and everyone around us to add spice to our lives. People are instrumental in how our prayers are answered. A smile from one, a word or two spoken from another, or a simple crush that cheers up your heart and gives you hope for another day.

Almost everyone we encounter fulfills a purpose, but not everyone we meet is meant to be our lifetime companion. Listen to the advice of your inner circle; they know you and see things from an unbiased perspective. It is a good idea to have your closest friends and family meet a potential mate and receive their feedback with an open mind and heart.

Develop and stay in a relationship where it flows. If you find yourself trying too hard to make things work with an individual, you are wondering if they could be "the one," trying too hard is your answer. No, that person is not "the one" for you. A good relationship flows easily. If something is bothering you or not sitting right, ask yourself why. What are your deal breakers? Compose a list of your dream partner and keep that somewhere close, maybe in your Bible. Here's a big reveal: a man or a woman who consistently disrespects you in words or deeds, such as not honoring your values, is not someone for you.

When God responds to your specific prayers and inquiries about your life and your future, believe Him. Hold tight to His promises to you. "But these things I plan won't happen right away. Slowly, steadily, surely, the time approaches when the vision will be fulfilled. If it seems slow, do not despair, for these things will surely come to pass. Just be patient! They will not be overdue a single day" (Habakkuk 2:3 TLB)!

Never be afraid to let people go if they're not right; often,
that's the only way you can make room for the right person.

—STUART WILDE

CHAPTER 20

Change with Courage

"Lord, grant me the wisdom to release what I must and the courage to move into the unknown with faith that I will be shown my way each day."

—CAROLINE MYSS

Transition was on the horizon in more ways than one. God's promises were given to me. I knew I would serve Him with someone someday. After putting my face to the ground in prayer and crying for help in the midst of financial and emotional distress, God answered me with His scripture, Ruth 3:10-12.

I was heard. He had a man for my daughter and me, just like Ruth and her Boaz.

As this promise unfolded, I was in the process of walking through a conclusion to the whole Mr. Surveyor saga. This friendship was not a representation of my promised one. A purse with a proposal, promises to be taken care of, and a trip to Europe was pretty darn tempting—but our hearts know the way, and I'd released the relationship at the altar that day. A relationship where trust and respect do not reside is one I would not reside in.

A few days later, after my night shift, I picked up Jessica. We laughed during the ride home. I liked to get silly to make her laugh! Later in the day, I spent an hour with the Lord. I really missed Jessica, as the past two nights I'd had to work and was not able to have her home with me. I was sad, but I also knew I had no choice. This night shift job paid our rent; it was a blessing from God. I asked God to please do something. Could He do something about my heart's sadness, the yearning for family? I desired to stay home as a family, to be able to be a mother, student, and wife. I was thankful for the many blessings of the present, but I wanted that family. All would occur as it was meant to in God's time.

* * *

My friend Eileen—who ironically was introduced to me by Mr. Surveyor—told me straight out one day, "Mr. Surveyor is not for you and all the rest of our group agrees." She asked if she could share my number with a friend at the Police Department where she worked. He was going through a divorce and could use encouragement.

"Of course," I said. God had been using me to encourage lots of men. I laughed; I would have preferred some of them be "the one"!

She laughed with me and promised I would meet the right one when it was time.

Later that week, the phone rang. The man on the other end introduced himself as Scott Beck, Eileen's friend. He asked if I could share a little about myself. After the past few years and disappointments, I must admit, I came out strong with, "I am a Christian and go to church." He seemed intrigued because he asked me where I went. I said, "Morningside Church." Turns out, he'd just started going there.

My mouth dropped. Up to this point, every male friend I had ever met did not go to church, and I was used to sharing Jesus with them, except for Mr. Mercedes.

"Are you still there?" he asked.

"Yes, sorry. What service do you usually attend?"

"The first service."

Oh, my goodness. This guy went to church! And not any church, *my* church! And during the service we frequently attend.

He went on to say, "I think I know who you and your daughter are."

"Really?" How would he know who I was?

"Yes, you shared that you like to sit up front. Were you wearing a blue flowered dress last week?"

I had. *OH. MY. GOODNESS. What?!* "Well, please come up to me this Sunday and say hello. I look forward to meeting you."

He promised to do so, and we said goodbye. I couldn't concentrate for the rest of the day, and the conversation left me wondering.

When I picked Jessie up from her dad's that Saturday morning, I found out my poor baby had been sick since 4 a.m. I got my shift covered, and we spent the whole day together while I took care of her.

By Sunday, she was better, so we went to the 9 a.m. service, but I did not see Scott Beck. It was a wonderful service. It was the hardest week we have endured in quite a while, but God was doing work. Monday, I fasted. I went to Joyce's that evening. We spent a few hours praying and working through quite a bit.

* * *

By Wednesday that week, I felt stuck in my sadness. After work, I went home and cried. I literally could not look at my geography book. I had such a pain in my chest all week. I gave God my heart and all my emotions in prayer. We broke all walls and rebuked all fears, stress, anxiety, sadness, etc. I sought the Lord. I read His Word. I quoted and meditated on scriptures. "The Lord is my strength and my shield; My heart trusted in Him, and I am helped; therefore, my heart greatly rejoices, and with my song I will praise Him" (Psalm 28:7 NKJV).

By the next morning, all the pain in my chest was gone, and I had such peace! Scott continued to call, and we even exchanged a few emails. I liked talking to him, but we never met at church. After a few weeks of phone calls and emails, we set a date to meet at my favorite café, Osceola Café, in Downtown Stuart on a Thursday afternoon, September 19, 2002.

I was wearing my black jeans and purple striped, sleeveless sweater. I walked up to the front of the entrance, where he said he would be waiting, and sure enough, there was a man wearing serious black sunglasses with the sides covered as well. He was handsome. I was nervous.

"Scott?"

"Georgette?"

I think we may have shaken hands before entering the restaurant. They sat us at a table for two in front of the window overlooking the backside of the restaurant, where you could see the shops across the street and people walking by the window.

We both had a wonderful afternoon with lots of smiling and laughing. His eyes sparkled when he smiled, and I hadn't laughed like that in a while. On the way home, I called Eileen to tell her all about it.

"I owe you a hug. Thank you for connecting Scott and me," I said.

When I told my neighbors Lara and Kacey about our meeting, it turned out that Kacey worked with him. He was a sergeant for the Traffic Division. What a small world.

Eileen called me the next day to tell me Scott had gone to see her first thing that morning. He thanked her, too, telling her what a great time we had and how nice he thought I was.

Apparently, Scott, besides his serving the Lord, also had the Thomas Kinkade book I loved. I counted this as a sign. There was something about him, something good, and I felt good in his company, comfortable. I so wanted to do something special for him that would bring joy and brightness to his day. I went and picked out a card and assorted colored roses to have delivered to him at the Police Dept. the next day. They would surprise him, and I hoped they would lighten his heart a little.

Our emails back and forth continued.

During one of our evenings together, he said he was thankful God used Eileen to have us meet. He looked forward to a long, solid friendship, thanking me for my words of encouragement. He also said something about how being in company with a pretty woman meant so much to him. His words made me smile.

There was something *very* different about this friendship. I didn't know why or understand it then. He was currently not available any other way except as a friend. He needed to go through his divorce and then, depending on that outcome, heal. I felt peace in the relationship—peace for going forward, enjoying each moment of the friendship, looking forward to its growth, not totally questioning like I used to. I just sensed sweetness and peace. No doubts, no discomfort about it developing into something later. If that chapter were ever to come, we would look forward to it slowly, the pages turning.

It was a Wednesday afternoon when Scott called me next. He loved the flowers. They really touched him. We met for lunch and had a wonderful afternoon. Turns out, God used the flowers as a sign for Scott that I was someone meant for him. The timing of the flowers came after a serious prayer session he had with God.

We talked every day, and he was aware of what was occurring in my life, even remembering to ask how I did on my geography test. I was very excited about our next dinner plans.

Eileen shared again that Scott had all good things to say about me, which made me gleeful. She said that I was a girl with a huge heart and that I was deserving of his kindness.

Before youth service that same night, I lay on the floor just to be at God's feet. I was quiet. I was a little afraid. I thanked God for all he had done with us, for I truly was a totally new and different person. New thinking, new ways, new attitudes, and eyes opened to the truth. I thanked him so much for choosing to save me, to love me, and to teach, train, deliver, grow, and transform me through so very much. He remained with us always. I felt undeserving of His goodness and unworthy of such kindnesses. I was used to being ignored and working to get attention, which turned ugly. Thank the Lord for beauty, for ashes, and junk to jewels!

I felt many things, including a tenderness toward Scott, like we would "fit" together, I would be able to help him, support him, be his friend, and appreciate him. I thought of him often and liked to be in his company. I looked forward to meeting his daughters and getting to know him more. One evening, he came over to help me study for a geography assignment. It was hilarious! He spilled my wine all over my note cards and felt horrible, but we just laughed with each other.

He called me and left a message to say that he was thinking of me.

During this time, I even ended my friendship with Mr. Surveyor. The emotional stronghold that kept me in this unhealthy relationship had broken, and I realized even friendship was not healthy. I finally experienced full spiritual healing and freedom. I would be sad if he was hurt in any way, but he didn't truly love me. His love had been a selfish love, a flesh love. A lust love. If he truly had cared about me, about my welfare and feelings, he would have respected *my* boundaries and would have taken steps to be with me in a respectable, good way. This man had traits that were not healthy or safe. His spirit was not of God. All ties were cut.

* * *

Oh, my heart. My daughter was beginning to truly resent my working at night. Our schedule was getting to her and my not being more available. She desired me to be with her more.

Lord, reveal to me her hurts, resentments, wishes, desires, etc. Show me somehow, some way. I need to give her more of me and more fun quality times. She wants to go to Chuck E. Cheese. Lord, please help us. Yes, it's time for our routine to be changed a bit. Help somehow—a mate possibly—and give me support so I can be home more.

* * *

During my prayers, I asked God, "Who is Scott Beck? Who is he, Father?"

He seemed so tender, genuine, and caring. I loved that we'd met through a mutual friend, arranged just like I'd prayed for it! He was so kind to everyone, remembering their names and important events. He treated me like a lady and seemed sincere. I felt comfortable with him. I laughed so much with him. We were friends first, and I felt peace, no doubts about anything. He thought about us all the time. He was positive, happy, and chipper. I loved that we prayed together. Our relationship was in our Father's hands, to nurture and grow however He saw fit. He was so open with his feelings. I felt I could trust him. He said he would *never* cause me pain. He also looked very handsome in his uniform.

At Dillard's, we both had fun smelling colognes. I helped him pick out one, and he bought me perfume. He also got me a Godiva chocolate bar. What a sweetie.

We joked about "chocolate," an inside joke we now share together after I let him read my term paper about the experience I had with Mr.

Surveyor. I once compared sex acts with chocolate for a diabetic: feeling tempted by it but knowing we shouldn't have it. Sex before marriage is only enjoyable for the moment.

Shortly after this, I opened the door to find him standing there with a captivating bouquet of flowers and a bag of candy. As he handed me the candy, he asked if I liked this type. I looked down at the bag and saw peanut butter cups, my absolute favorites. I said yes, but he asked if I was sure. I looked at the bag again and noticed that they were sugar-free chocolates. Then it hit me. The man truly got it.

One may wonder why I would be vulnerable in that way. Why would I risk such a thing during the crucial courtship period? Good question! Usually, it was best-foot-forward, but not this time. I had learned a lot during the past few years. I was now determined, no matter what, that this southern Florida girl's values and morals would remain intact. I would remain true to myself. No more compromise, not this chick. I had learned from all the pain and now knew my value. I was leaving the bad memories and mistakes behind and moving forward but keeping all the lessons I'd learned. They had been hard-won! It was imperative that this man get this about me, my newly reconfirmed moral standards. If this were the man God had for me, the essay would not scare him off, but I was still anxious. Would he think I was a crazy person?

Apparently not! Not with him standing in the doorway and both of us laughing over a bag of sugar-free chocolates. We both knew exactly what that sugar-free chocolate was saying. Yes, he got it! This relationship was on a strict diet!

On a Monday night, Scott came over and cooked us linguine with shrimp and scallops and helped Jessie with her homework. Jessie thought he was "the one." She liked him a lot and, the night before, had even said she loved him. Things seemed just to be fitting in place.

🪨 JEWELS ⬤

Truth sinks in slowly. All your a-ha moments do matter. They build up inside you. You review all the facts and observations as you become aware of them. It all matters. You gain the courage to change. You can keep banging your head on the wall of a particular relationship, but a person is who they are. Believe what they do, not what they say. When a man brings you gifts with the expectation of immediate physical affection, understand how inappropriate this is. You deserve better. A man of integrity blesses you with gifts with no strings attached. Wait for the man who is approved and blessed by God. This man is a great man. How to know if a man is for you? Do they respect you? Do they respect your boundaries? Yes? Keep getting to know each other. No? Run! And run right after a disrespect occurs.

Another sign a man is not a good fit for you is when something occurs in your life, and you need encouragement or help, but they don't show up for you—hard pass! A person who cares about you will show up when you need them. They will care about your heart and your feelings. The man with good intentions thinks about you often and wants to speak with you. He will call you daily. The man God selected for me called me several times a day, brought me coffee, cooked delicious meals, and when I needed help with something, he was always available. He respected boundaries, too. Make your list of the man your heart desires. Knowing what you do want and knowing what you do not want is vital. Honor yourself and your kids. If you feel cherished and respected, then your kids will be cherished and respected.

Keep journaling or talking to yourself out loud, too. You will eventually hear yourself loud and clear and take the necessary steps to implement change in your life. Even if you have to crawl, like I did, toward the right decisions and actions. Ladies, you deserve the complete package. Don't settle! I had to shut the door so the right door could open for me. And this happened to me once my heart's intentions for a different path took shape. When in doubt, don't. Your gut will tell you the truth. Listen to it. Instead of trying to speak your desires into action, create your plan of action and implement it. Maybe you will plan to have dates with friends every night during the month. Or maybe you can agree with a friend to text them when you feel tempted to call the person you know is not meant for you.

All your efforts to learn about yourself and your family's history will help you. God desires to break all generational patterns leading to death and sorrow. He desires to develop all new patterns for you and future generations, leading to life and joy! Desire the Heaven on Earth marriage or relationship.

When you marry, you don't just marry the man; you marry their parents, children, ex-spouse, and friends. If there are a lot of complications, decide if these are manageable.

Even with hindsight, I wouldn't change anything; I needed to walk through every single experience. It was these experiences, circumstances, and people that made it possible for me to realize God's truth for me. I had to awaken myself from within. The proper insight that moved me to proper decisions and choices came only after receiving spiritual, emotional, and physical examples, guidance, and incidents. Sharing my junk with you is embarrassing now, for it would seem obvious what I needed to have done. But it is true: One cannot judge another for their journey unless they, too, walked in the same shoes. And this is impossible, for each of us shows up in life from vastly different backgrounds, experiences, family dynamics, education, upbringing, and communities with our own perspectives. I was naïve, young, emotionally immature, and wounded. God's ways are higher than ours, and it is useless to try to understand them. God knew what He was doing. I had only a tiny glimpse and recognition of what was occurring within my heart and spirit. When one experiences abandonment and rejection, it goes deep. Add a few generations of families experiencing the same heart wounds, and it goes even deeper into our psyche.

Years later, during my master's degree studies, I completed a genogram. What an eye-opener! Amy Marschall, PsyD, in a February 14, 2022, *Very Well Mind* article, describes genograms as a visual representation of a person's family, the relationships between members, and medical and mental health histories. Genograms reveal transgenerational patterns and make connections between interactions between relatives. Individuals may also identify how various patterns in their family history impact their current relationships and/or observe how intergenerational trauma might be affecting them. My genogram may have been useful to me during my single mom years, but God brings truth to us when we can handle it and are ready to try and change. I was not able to sever the physical connection I experienced with Mr. Surveyor. It was extremely familiar to where I had come from. I was used to holding on to things for fear of abandonment, just for the sake of keeping them. This included staying friends with people who did not deserve my friendship. I had not known greater intimacy until God used these situations to bring about my inner healing. It was only after this that my caboose, as I called the part of me still unable or unwilling to grasp new truth and way of being, finally caught up to where my heart and head were directing my steps in alignment with God's guidance.

So, please, do not be as hard on yourself as I was throughout my whole single mom season. If I could change anything, it would be that. I wish I could have had more love and grace toward myself. Growth occurs when we do not give up. Be gracious with yourself. You are precious and beloved, and in time, your caboose will eventually catch up to where your heart desires you to be. Everything will connect and come together like it did for me, in your perfect way and in perfect timing. Trust me. Do not give up on yourself. I'm not saying you get a free pass for continually putting yourself in dangerous situations harmful to your heart or spirit; I am saying keep asking for help. Keep working. Decide to meet as many healthy people as you can. Join clubs, groups, and organizations that aspire to a greater good. The faith community is a positive and impactful one to participate in. Take music lessons or join a painting or dance class. Take part in your community to benefit from human connections. This is life-changing!

And sometimes, when you begin to change, you will receive it back.

Manipulators are good at keeping people in line with their preferences. Mr. Surveyor had no desire to change his ways but did desire for me to remain in his life in ways beneficial to him. I can't tell you how many women I've known who stay in relationships too long with someone who is not in alignment with their higher selves. No one should waste their life by settling for less than what they want in a relationship. Dear one, you are so much more worthy and deserving than this. Yes, it will take risks, and you will have to walk through a scary season of the unknown. Maybe you will feel lonely for a season. But what if your perfect partner is just around that scary corner? I'd say you're worth the risk and taking that leap of faith.

Follow your heart. God leads you with your heart. He places those dreams within. Trust God. He will guide you in His amazing ways with His lavish love. Be your own bestie and try to do what you would advise your loved ones to do. Hugs to you, because even though it is hard, it is so worth it. Make room in your life to exchange your junk for jewels, and watch your jewels sparkle before your eyes.

We are born into a life. The life is waiting there. We don't pick it; we step into it—parents, firstborn or last, the part of the country, the part of the world, our appearance, the efficiency of our brain. Then, a time comes when we realize that we also have choices, and so we begin the task of building our own life—an impossible task considering the number of days we are given to complete it. However, I don't think that's important; what is important is to begin.

—HUGH PRATHER

CHAPTER 21

Courtship

"Home is where the heart is, the soul's bright guiding star. Home is where real love is, where our own dear ones are. Home means someone waiting to give a welcome smile. Home means peace and joy and rest and everything worthwhile."

—ANONYMOUS

God, Scott seems to fit just so with us. Can I start to get excited? Should I still hold off? Refrain? Wait and see? All will be well if this is YOUR doing. So far, it appears to be so. Show us, please. We love you and are yours. God, I thank you for being in our lives. Words could never express it. I am blessed to be touching lives and helping others through ministry. Thank you for changing us and for our hope and our future in you!

Scott called first thing in the morning, and Jessie and I met up with him after I picked her up. We had fun visiting, laughing, and smiling, all while standing in a shopping plaza parking lot.

When I was hugging him goodbye, I said, "I love you." Oh, my goodness! I was surprised myself—I couldn't imagine what he must be thinking. The words just spurted out! He chuckled and smiled, rather enjoying my embarrassment. There was absolutely no expectation for these words from me or from him, for we were in the early stages of our friendship. I may have been surprised, but I did not feel bad, nor did he make me feel bad. We both believed in the power of our hearts, and the heart knows things before we do at times.

I left smiling, enjoying our time and wanting to be with him. He made my heart smile. No nervousness or doubts—just comfort and compatibility. Things seemed to connect.

He brought me dinner, and it was nice to be thought of. We sat on the porch and talked till he had to leave to get his daughter, Brittany, and I had to go to work. I believe feelings had been developing since our first meeting.

* * *

One night, Scott came over after 8:30 p.m. We sat on the porch, sipped wine, and talked for hours. I felt good in his arms. No guilty feelings. We want to do things right.

Another night, an amazing thing happened at the end of our time together. I was having serious thoughts, debating whether to share them, when he noticed and asked what I was thinking. I shared painful memories of my past marriage and how I had felt ignored. I asked him to assure me that no matter how busy he got, he'd never ignore me.

He was amazed, for at that same moment, he was having the same thoughts. He hugged me and said he would never do that. I would never have to shout to receive attention and regard.

* * *

After one of our coffee dates, as I walked out to my car in the parking lot, I realized I had a flat. Not fun! Well, Scott was such a sweetie, and he changed it for me. (Thank goodness my tire went flat in the parking lot!) Mid-day, Scott called and asked if I had taken care of the tire yet, and I said I was going to make calls after Jessica and I finished playing school. He said he already made the calls and asked if it would be alright if he and Brittany stopped by and if she could play with Jessica while he took care of the tire.

I asked, "What is the damage?" He said we would talk later.

They stopped by after I had started working on my paperwork. Both Scott and Brittany were amazed at the pile of paper and things I was going through. The girls played in Jessie's room while I got everything organized and sorted. I was able to pay some bills but was still behind on others, including the car payment.

He took care of the car for me. He put two new tires on the front! I hugged and kissed him thank you! A $150 gift for us. We were grateful. Scott stayed until we had to drop Jessie off at her dad's. We had such a pleasant time visiting and talking.

* * *

Scott came over one Tuesday after work. When he walked up our stairs, I was sitting with a little girl on my lap, comforting her and her mother, who were both crying. I gave the little girl a stuffed animal I had, trying to soothe her. The woman had been a mail-order bride and was living with a neighbor, one I didn't associate with. Her little girl couldn't stop crying, and the man had told her mother to get the child to stop crying or leave. I tried to help them by making a few calls the next day.

Scott told me he loved me. Seeing me with the little girl on my lap, loving on her and providing comfort, was a defining moment for him. It was then he knew how he felt about me.

How do I love thee? Let me count the ways.

—ELIZABETH BARRETT BROWNING

Scott had a vision during a prayer session—he and I were off to one side, side by side. All peace. Off to another side was his very soon-to-be ex-wife and the man she cheated on him with, the other man's wife crying behind them with sadness and turmoil.

Scott had his final divorce hearing. It was a very emotional day for him, but the door had shut. The deal was done. Later that day, he received sad news about a man he went to training school with. He had been ambushed and murdered, and Scott was going to attend the funeral services. The official death of his marriage and the death of a dear friend were two devastating blows in a matter of hours.

* * *

Jessica, who still desperately wished for a sibling and a family, had been crying. She told me she was lonely and wanted Brittany to be her family. I told her I believe God may be hooking her up on this one.

* * *

Scott and I went to Downtown Stuart where my favorite shops and restaurants were located. We had coffee and appetizers, watched a movie about an artist named Henri Louver, and then a gentlemen lectured afterward. It was fascinating and interesting. There was a moment during the film where it was so special, so intense. I was holding Scott's hands, tracing them, looking at them. I had a "knowing" feeling. These were the hands of the man for us. My Boaz.

He took me to dinner afterward. We had fun, and Scott and I cracked up laughing about how the waiter flirted with me. I wore a purple dress he'd bought me. I love it.

* * *

Our relationship was progressing well. Anytime there was uncertainty, God seemed to bring confirmation for the two of us to continue getting to know each other. I will always remember the evening we were listening to my music CD from the 1995 film *Dangerous Minds*. I was sharing how Michelle Pfeiffer's character, a teacher, stood out to me and how I believed the same about difficult youth or people in general. There are reasons people act the way they do. Scott had immediate strong opposing thoughts more on the justice only side of things, and our debate did not end well.

It was the first time we'd fought, and I think we both expected not to see each other again. Until the next morning when I found his birth certificate in the file folder he had left on my kitchen counter. He had been in the process of obtaining a passport earlier during the day before he stopped by to see me. When he first arrived and walked into my apartment, I remember him having to finish sorting paperwork in a file folder before we sat on the couch together. God definitely enjoys being humorous. Right there, in black and white, were the names of Scott's parents, and when I read the name of his mom, I couldn't believe it! Her name was Ruth. I can't remember which one of us made the phone call, me to tell him he forgot some important documents or him to ask if he could pick up his papers. I think we even laughed about his forgetting them and forcing our next communication! And I'm sure I shared the significance of learning about his late mom's first name and what it meant. Both of us believed in signs and understood how God guides our steps.

Our Valentine's Day was epic. It was amazingly beautiful, but throughout the day, I felt a little emotional. Afraid. We had a romantic evening at the Osceola Café, and I surprised Scott; Beth, the owner at the time, helped me. The singers called Scott up in front of everyone and handed him the guitar I bought him. Everyone clapped and took our picture. Scott and I enjoyed a delicious dinner. Earlier in the day, he'd even treated me to a hair appointment and manicure. Then, at the restaurant, he gifted me chocolate and perfume—a giant bottle of Truth. I felt so special and cared for, valued in the way I'd been dreaming about for years.

That night we also talked about the future. Scott shared that he had almost experienced homelessness a few times during his separation and single time, bouncing from place to place. When it was possible, he was keen on finding a new home. He invited me to join him in house hunting because he envisioned his future with Jessica and I joining him and his daughters.

The no pre-marital sex was one boundary Scott and I both agreed that we would never cross, or it meant the end of our relationship. But boy did we kiss for hours and hours. No joke, and he was a great kisser—and still is!

JEWELS

When your "Boaz" arrives, set your boundary as high as possible. For, as one of our pastors once shared, whatever your boundary or standard is, you will fall just under it. Good advice.

And ladies, this bears repeating: one sure-fire way to know if someone is "the one" is to ask yourself if your boundaries and values are respected.

Enjoy every moment of your courtship. Soak it all in. Capture the memories with your camera and your journal. Remember, there are many seasons in our lives. Your courtship period is really important. It is laying the foundation of your relationship and future together as a couple. Getting to know someone takes time. Take the time to get to know each other well. Take all your concerns to God every step of the way. God will respond and confirm your forward motion step by step. Circumstances will work themselves out. You will gain a knowing if the person is meant for you.

When God reveals His truth to your concerns and prods you forward, trust Him. And then trust your prospective partner and your relationship together. If you cannot trust the one you are in courtship with, that's your answer. No trust and no security mean no faith.

In faith, take the leap. Commit. "To say that one waits a lifetime for his soulmate to come around is a paradox. People eventually get sick of waiting, take a chance on someone, and by the art of commitment, become soulmates, which takes a lifetime to perfect" (Criss Jami).

I don't need to completely understand the big picture to know that my role is important. I don't have to know the destination to know I'm headed in the right direction. Though I may not know where I am going, I'm not lost; I am exploring.

—JANA STANFIELD

CHAPTER 22

Commitment

"You always have two choices: your commitment versus your fear."

—SAMMY DAVIS, JR.

My prayers changed. My heart became concerned and fearful. I became more aware of my weaknesses, sins, and failures. I was afraid of leaving our safe, peaceful abode to venture out into the unknown. New "friends" seemed to settle in: apprehension and anxiety!

The mail was full of God's answers to me, His Words.

My grandmother Hopkins sent an Easter card with a little card in it that said: "Optimism's positive thinking lit up," and "Hold an image of the life you want, and that image will become fact."

Dave Wilkerson's newsletter came in—perfect timing, as always—explaining giving understanding, peace, guidance, help, and describing miracles and "the unrelenting love of God." We can't change our natural tendency toward sin, but we can receive Christ's nature by faith.

I received a letter from the pastor's wife with encouraging words.

Allen, my friend from Lucio's, sent a letter sharing a song he heard, maybe for our wedding: "Tell me what you thought about when you were gone and so alone. The worst is over; you can have the best of me. We got older, but we're still young. We never grew out of this feeling. We just won't give up." He says it really summed me up. That I always give "the best of me" and show such enthusiasm for life that although "we get older," we feel like we're still young. He says it is most definitely a picture of who I am. "What's cool is there is still so much more about you that words or lyrics couldn't tell!" he wrote. He looked forward to our eventual engagement and wedding.

April 20, 2003, and we celebrated Christ having risen! Lately, it seemed that more of my not-so-good side had come out in my relationship with Scott. I didn't react well; my perspective had changed. The early days of courtship were now intertwined with our doing life together from separate households with our different calendars full of obligations, responsibilities all navigated with our two different personalities and communication styles. Real-life moved into our bubble of romance and fun. Scott and I both became more defensive. Maybe we both wanted to hold tight to our independence and freedoms gained through the healings obtained from our painful divorces.

As time progressed, I saw all sides of Scott, including his faults, as he was now seeing mine. Of course, we continued to believe with all our hearts that God brought us together to answer our prayers for a new beginning with someone. Yes, we were confident in God's selections for ourselves and our girls, especially since, after great moments of doubt and uncertainty, God seemed to show us something specific that kept our steps moving forward together. Let's face it, though. We are merely human, and fear is alive and well, and commitment to another is a serious decision. There was much at stake for all of us, and neither of us wished to experience the pain we had from our divorces and absolutely wished to protect our girls. Faith asks us to trust. To love another involves massive risk and trust. I know each of us found beautiful peace and joy in our solo lives with our Jesus. The fear of losing this treasure scared each of us. Walking by faith relies on our heart walk with

God, and the more time we spend reading His Word and praying, the more we understand His personal plan for our lives. Our hearts and intuition were relied on, for this is how God directed our daily steps and decisions.

> *God, help me. I guess there would be no man totally perfect, BUT I am thinking a man who was more mature in the fruits would not swear. Set me straight, God, for I am not perfect, and I can see how very narrow-minded I am. Forgive me, help me, change me, and give me your perspective. God, WHERE do you want me? Where do you want Jessie and me?*

> *God, I am JUST NOT sure today if my being one with Scott is something that will make us both better in you. Show me, God. Lately, we have been bringing out the worst in each other. I enjoy my freedom, but I also enjoy being with Scott.*

> *God, help me. I choose to let go of what I need to let go of. God, I need more perspective on this. Please, somehow, hook me up with people you desire to share with me. God, show me your heart. Can I love this man unconditionally? Can I be more unselfish? More considerate of others? Submissive to you and him?*

* * *

And God responds yet again through our church sermon notes on May 11, 2003.

LIVING A LIFE OF FAITH, LIVING THE BETTER LIFE, PART 4

Trust in the Lord with ALL your heart and lean not on your own understanding; in all your ways acknowledge Him, and He will make your paths straight. Proverbs 3:5-6 (NIV)

Trust in the Lord with all your heart.

We specifically pray and ask. He specifically answers.

"There is risk in each stroke of your ax!" Ecclesiastes 10:8 (TLB)

Trust involves risk in *every* step.

Relationships are one of the *most* difficult things but also a great blessing.

"Love the Lord your God with all your heart and with all your soul and with all your mind and with all your strength." Mark 12:30 (NIV)

"If you try to KEEP your life for yourself, you will lose it. But if you give up your life for Me, you will find true life." Matthew 16:25 NLT

I received what God was sharing. Would I trust God or trust myself? He says to lean not on your own understanding. I thought I knew what was good for me. I put myself in boxes, having my own end in mind. I had to get out of this box, knowing that He knows better for me. I had to do the 80 percent that was clear, and He would reveal the other 20 percent to me. A person of faith sees the glass firmly in the hands of God, not half full or half empty.

"Taste and see that the Lord is good. Oh, the joys of those who trust in Him!" Psalm 34:8 (NLT)

"O my soul, don't be discouraged. Don't be upset. Expect God to act." Psalm 42:11 (TLB)

"He is a faithful God, who keeps His promise and is merciful to thousands of generations of those who love Him and obey His Commandments." Deuteronomy 7:9 (GW)

"Trust God from the bottom of your heart; don't try to figure out everything on your own. Listen for God's voice in everything you do, everywhere you go; He's the one who will keep you on track." Proverbs 3:5-6 (MSG)

God would rather have me struggle to give 100 percent of myself to Him, and this did not mean a perfect life or a relationship. It meant I get from point A to B—it would work. Now, there are things I need to give to God in the present. Deciding to obey God can be hard, but it will lead to lasting happiness. I needed to leave my human reasoning at the door; He knew my heart. He knew what I needed.

Scott and I knew a long courtship period was not going to be feasible. To confirm our path, we decided to pursue pre-marriage counseling.

Another small world piece of information Scott and I discovered about each other was when he learned of my last name. It seemed familiar to him. He recalled having worked on a criminal case involving my ex-husband and his wife, Delilah. Her son shot two people. Scott knew about me before even meeting me.

* * *

God continued to be quick to respond to any feelings of being overwhelmed or unsure. "Lord, I am overwhelmed, please come to my help" (Isaiah 38:14b NJB). "God sent the angel Gabriel … to a virgin named Mary. She was engaged to be married to a man named Joseph … Gabriel appeared to her and said, 'Greetings, favored woman! The Lord is with you!' Confused and disturbed, Mary tried to think what the angel could mean. "Don't be frightened. Mary," the angel told her, 'For God has decided to bless you'" (Luke 1:26-30 NLT).

Life is out of our control, and we are not going to figure it all out. I needed to let go of my need to control situations, for there were and were going to be many uncontrollable situations. I don't have to worry. God is in control. God can do anything, and He says He will work out His plans for our lives. "Mary asked the angel, 'BUT HOW can I have a baby? I am a virgin' … the angel replied … 'Nothing is impossible with God!'" Luke 1:34 & 37 NLT) "Mary responded, 'I am the Lord's servant, and I AM WILLING TO ACCEPT whatever He wants. May everything you have said come true.' (Luke 1:38 NLT)." "Trust God from the bottom of your heart; don't try to figure out everything on your own" (Proverbs 3:5 MSG). "The Lord will work out His plans for my life" (Psalm 138:8 NLT).

More encouragement came my way, with the message clear: "Let others help me." I can relax and stop being overwhelmed. Just like Mary, I need to trust. God encourages us along the way, even when we are on a difficult path. God will give us strength. "You are blessed for believing that the Lord would keep His promise to you" (Luke 1:45 GW).

* * *

In my Tuesday Bible study, someone said, "God is going to give you your heart's desires." For me, that meant more of God. She sensed such agape love. She saw a river flowing, blue water, and interpretation.

I mused afterward and realized: I was hooked up heart to heart … heart to heart with God, heart to heart with Scott. The second chance I had prayed for, God's promise to me through the scripture Ruth 3:10-11 was coming to pass.

Through my daily devotions, I was receiving other discernment. We were heading into strange territory (Joshua 3:1-13). God does not ask us to go where He does not lead. And He said to me, "My grace is sufficient for you, for My strength is made perfect in weakness." "Therefore, most gladly I will rather boast in my infirmities, that the power of Christ may rest upon me" (2 Corinthian 12:9 NKJV).

I think I was understanding. God goes before us, and He will never leave us or forsake us. This was a transition we were in. Scott and I had been dating for almost ten months. God truly had hooked us up, heart to heart!

My love continued to grow for Scottie, and he made a comment: "As fear diminishes, it becomes more obvious." And I woke up with a scripture: "Be still and know that I am God" (Psalm 46:10 NKJV).

∗ ∗ ∗

Scott and I had been dating for eleven months. My heart was afraid of my walk with God changing within the transition of Scott's and my relationship. On Labor Day 2003, I knew it was a day of new beginnings (Ephesians 1:17-23). It was time to go forward and look up and forward like a flint.

As I sang and prayed in the Spirit, it became such a pretty song in melody. I did not know the words, but God comforted me, "**There, there, there, sweet, sweet, precious, precious child, there, there, sweet, etc.,**" over and over. It was soothing.

Scott and I celebrated our one-year dating anniversary at our favorite place, Osceola Café, at the table—our table— where we first met.

God sent imagery while I was praying by the oceanside about the sand, how all of it together just looks like sand, but each tiny particle, when observing it closer, sparkles, really sparkles, like diamonds. And God said we sparkle like that, all the stuff around, but inside, we sparkle like that to Him. I must remember to just do it, little by little, and it will get done. Every day, every step, just keep moving.

All of life is a process; like the ants, little by little, they do so very much, but if you just looked at the one, you would see nothing. But if you looked at what each of them accomplished over time, it's amazing what it adds up to.

$$* * *$$

Scott proposed to me on Christmas Day in front of my mom, dad, sisters, and Jessica. I said, "yes." It was time to leave Jesus', Jessie's, and my love nest. "Commitment is what transforms a promise into a reality" (Abraham Lincoln).

God had restored the years. "I will restore to you the years that the swarming locust has eaten" (Joel 2:25). No matter how dark your past, with Christ, your future is bright.

This had been a year of much transition and change as we prepared to leave our home of almost seven years. Our 1507 apartment, the place God brought us to, the place God loved on us so, the place we received so much healing, so many conversations between God and me, so many prayers of seed planted, now coming to fruition. Scott was our Boaz. He was that man God promised to us years ago. A man after God's own heart. He was God's perfect gift to us. Our wedding ceremony was held on May 22, 2004.

JEWELS

Coming to the point of commitment takes time. Trusting in the Lord also takes time, and once you find yourself there, you come to trust in your relationship with the Lord. This includes how God responds to your heart matters. You come to know God's ways with you personally, up close and personal. You learn to count on God to help you and guide you. Your life seasons do change, and how God responds to you may also change, but rest assured your relationship remains intact. God guides you step by step, and He never abandons His kids. Even when I started to revert to past behaviors or fearful thinking, God revealed Himself to me in the circumstance. Leaving the nest is a scary contemplation. Leaving a place where you may have come to know unconditional love for the very first time is not something you ever imagined having to do. But this is what I learned. A place is just that: a place. God is not restricted by place. He never was. "Therefore, the Lord Himself will give you a sign; The virgin will conceive, and give birth to a Son, and will call Him Emmanuel" (NIV). "Emmanuel" literally means "with us is God" or "God with us." Jennifer Slattery sums this up for us; "In truth, God is and always has been *with* us. He is omnipresent, which means He is everywhere all the time. Speaking of God, the ancient psalmist David wrote, *"Where can I go from Your Spirit? Where can I flee from Your presence? If I go up to the heavens, You are there; if I make my bed in the depths, You are there. If I rise on the wings of the dawn, if I settle on the far side of the sea, even there Your hand will guide me, Your right hand will hold me fast"* (Psalm 139:7-10 NIV)."

Dear one, your heart is safe with God. Once you learn how to hear from God and walk in His ways, you will gain confidence in discerning His revelations for you and begin to understand how He guides you. You not only change with courage but step by step in faith during your courtship, and finally, it takes courage to commit. Yes, even when all the lovey-dovey feelings are present, when some of those lovey-dovey feelings diminish in the face of true personalities that differ from yours, and especially when it becomes obvious your nest departure draws nigh. God knew I would need extra assurances to leave our peaceful abode, and He provided them.

Difficulties in relationships do not necessarily mean the relationship is no good. Life has difficulties daily and times when God has us in difficult seasons. This does not mean we are being punished. Life can be hard, but God helps us through every single time.

God made it clear that Scott was the "Boaz" He promised for me and my daughter. Having love and romance does not mean we will not experience unloving moments with one another. God is with us and in all situations. I came to understand how crucial our courtship period was. Our "promised land" is a land that must be taken. When the Israelites were about to cross over into their promised land, land God had planned for them to have, Moses sent scouts in to look and to report their findings upon their return. "Then I said to you, 'You have reached the hill country of the Amorites, which the Lord our God is giving us. ²¹ See, the Lord your God has given you the land. Go up and take possession of it as the Lord, the God of your ancestors, told you. Do not be afraid; do not be discouraged'" (Deuteronomy 1:21-22 NIV).

The scouts all reported that everything was exactly as God promised. There were delicious fruits and luscious foliage. The land was good. The only problem was there were giants already residing there. All the scouts but two suggested they find another way to their promised land. Two believed God at His Word and said God would be with us as we conquer these individuals that displeased God. God blessed them, and they got to see and live in God's promised land. The other scouts died in the wilderness due to their unbelief.

Your second chance in a new relationship will have its challenges. Lots of them. All relationships take daily work and life has good and hard moments to navigate through. As much as I wish it were so, Hallmark stories are just that, stories, and not reality. There are mixed blessings in life. The good news is you will not be alone in navigating life's daily decisions, delights, or detriments.

Lord, I put to prayer all of us, our lives, our hopes, dreams, abilities, and weaknesses. Help us be effective and victorious. God, please, in spite of my failures, will you PLEASE be visible in our lives, our plans? Please take control, take charge of our days. Please put together ALL of the details and plans for the wedding, for moving into the house, for all of the needed items, for the new home, furnish us with a place to go for our honeymoon, touch all of us— develop special bonds between the girls and me. Bless our relationships. Let our relationships be sweet from your touches—special beyond special, let us love each other, help each other understand and be gracious toward each other.

Commitment turns a promise into reality with words that speak boldly of your intentions and actions that speak louder than words.

—STEVE BRUNKHORST

Epilogue

God's love for you and me never ends. His love pours out like a waterfall: continuous, lavish, and joyous.

Dear precious one, stop beating yourself up for your failures and things you have not been able to change. For whatever reason, there are circumstances that we find ourselves in that we need to ride out. And it may be bigger than us. All we can do is look to God and do our best to follow His will. And never stop asking for help. Lots of help. Do what you know and can do, and God will do the rest. Keep showing up. Keep writing in your journal, going to Church and Bible studies and other support groups. Add it all to your schedule as much as can fit peacefully. Trust what comes to your heart to check out or learn more about. Pay attention. This is not an accident. This is on purpose. Truth sets us free and comes to us in a variety of ways: through our Bible reading, our devotions, books, conversations, radio, podcasts, or any random thing coming across your path. God will remain faithful, no matter how much time goes by. God is faithful and longsuffering. He is a God of compassion. He knows of our weakness. He knows why we fail and desires to heal us. He will heal every single piece if we remain in Him and allow His touches and tweaks, however painful. As painful as sharing this story is, it is eye-opening, not just in the shock of how drastic the truth seemed to contrast with my continuously perceived wrong actions or choices made. God was doing His thing behind the scenes. He added different people and situations into my life that were bringing me higher and higher on the mountaintop, away from the valley of brokenness toward the mountain of victory. One piece, one touch, one truth at a time. There were moments when I understood this, and it was too much to comprehend His great love for me. His love is what changed me and helped me. His love is what will help you, too. Whatever you need, He knows. His methods of peeling back the layers and adding newness to our lives are mysterious and magnificent. If I were stronger and healthier, I would have made many different choices. But I was not. There were things occurring within me that were beyond my understanding. The healing needed to come from God. No matter what right choices I could have made instead, there was still something that needed His special touch. And there are some healings that continue throughout our lifetime, layer by layer, circumstance by circumstance. God will never give up on us.

Write out your dreams. You may have no idea at the beginning of your healing journey, but as you progress, you will discover new places, people, interests, and hobbies that interest you. Find ways to do them. Remember, my daughter and I went to the library and fed our minds and hearts and dreams for free. Books, music CDs, etc. The beach was our place that fed our souls and hearts and brought joy every single time. Then the river, too. Find your place and go. Visiting nature brings peace and joy, and it is free! I would take art lessons for fun. They have community classes with your Parks and Recreation. Attend plays and musicals if you love that. I did, and it changed me for the better. DREAM BIG. There are no limits to what your heart can desire!

God does not always feel about us the way we feel about ourselves, especially when we mess up. Read His Word, and you will see that. Look at the people He chose.

Epilogue

You may have heard "smell the roses," or "embrace the moment," or "there is only the present." Truly understand how fast time goes. You will never have your present moment to do over. Your time as a single may be a short or long time. This is different for each of us. Maybe some of you never wish to marry or get into a relationship with another person. This could be true. Maybe you are like me and hoped from day one of your singlehood for a second chance at romance. Either way, one never knows. There have been folks who swore off love, but when the right person came along, they found themselves in a new relationship. This is why, no matter where your heart is at this moment in time, know what your priorities are and be diligent in focusing on them daily. My daughter was my priority. She came first. But then there came the necessity to earn income. But one job, not even two jobs, brought in enough income for us to live adequately, never mind keep our housing and food in the fridge. But if I could do it all over again, I would never stop asking for help. This includes staying connected to individuals who offer sound wisdom in various aspects of life. I am sure if I had taken time to ask professionals and more spiritual folks about keeping my daughter in her Christian private school or enrolling her in public school, we may have experienced a whole set of different circumstances. Maybe we would have found more time to be together. Maybe. One does not know this to be true. I still carry the pain associated with this, and I have worked hard to let it go with God's help. My heart still grieves at the loss of time with my daughter, and we both hurt from this and carry wounds. Please do yourself a favor and take time to gain counsel throughout your journey on anything that may pop up in your life. God does speak of sound counsel being a good thing.

Praying about everything is your lifesaver. God always provides the best counsel. He promises, too, and He comes through. "The Lord gives sight to the blind, the Lord lifts up those who are bowed down, the Lord loves the righteous" (Psalm 146:8 NIV). Beautiful one, you are God's precious opal. Sparkle brightly.

I learned that my "happy" is my joy in the Lord! "Then he said to them, 'Go your way, eat the fat, drink the sweet, and send portions to those for whom nothing is prepared; for this day is holy to our Lord. Do not sorrow, for the joy of the Lord is your strength'" (Nehemiah 8:10 NKJV). "So the ransomed of the Lord shall return, and come to Zion with singing, with everlasting joy on their heads. They shall obtain joy and gladness; Sorrow and sighing shall flee away" (Isaiah 51:11 NKJV). My joy is from my heart-to-heart relationship with God. I pray and read my Bible daily, and I continue to pray about everything and everyone. All my dreams and desires are prayed for and written about in my journal. God and I have verbal and written conversations, with me talking to Him and writing to Him in my journal. "Delight yourself also in the Lord, and He shall give you the desires of your heart" (Psalm 37:4 NKJV).

You are never too old to set a new goal or
to dream a new dream.

—C.S. LEWIS

Acknowledgments

My *Junk to Jewels* journey, from brokenness and despair to beauty and delight, was a lovely, painful, God-orchestrated one, full of divine appointments and serendipity. My daughter and I are forever blessed by all the people who came into our lives.

Junk to Jewels is a story of hope, inspiration, and new beginnings. And I have discovered a scenario that plays out on repeat throughout our journey here on Earth. Each of us experiences various seasons of life, and when we enter a new season, we may find ourselves in a junk stage again as God works through new and old issues that pop up in the new circumstances. The miraculous use of people, places, and things to speak to us astounds me. God uses people in such profound ways as His arms and feet. I could not be who I am today without every single woman and man who took the time to show kindness to Jessie and me. God was strategic in His rescue mission, and place was of utmost importance. Pinewood Pointe Apartment community during our time there was a charming place comprised of beautiful neighbors. Gratitude never leaves our hearts for the rich friendships created with our building neighbors: Tom and Julia, Kacey and Lara, Stephanie and Drew, Mike, and Don and his daughter. The community at large also brought good friends into our lives and many fun moments were had together: Alicia and Tyler, Toni and Jordania, Barry and his boys, Ida, Greg and Carly, June, and many others who came and went during our residency. After our home of the heart was secured, God placed us in a spiritual home, one that remained our church family for twenty years. Thank you, Morningside Church family, all our brothers and sisters in Christ—each of you shone brightly for the Kingdom in your embracing us and keeping us until our broken selves healed. Then, my heart knew great joy as I learned how to serve the King with such gracious, excellent, humble servants. I knew love because each of you loved my daughter and me. I wish I could list every single person's name who impacted our lives in some way, but word count is limited. In my Bible, I have two names written as my Spiritual Mommas, a high honor: Miss Margaret Ruplin and Miss Joyce Hietala. Miss Carol Natiello, Miss Joan Happ, Miss Anna Steakin, Melody Hearn, and Ilsa Rauschen were other eagles looking out after the eaglets. These women never tired or tarried in responding to God's leading of His girls. They never turned away from our ugly. Ladies' Bible Study started off in Miss Margaret's penthouse and grew from a few women to a church sanctuary full of spiritual warriors. I love you all. Dear sisters and friends Lisa Ronkko, Tracy Savoia, Vanessa Rinehart, Lisa Henrichs, Lori Gagne, and Karen Barr, what a joy to do life and grow together in the Lord. I am blessed to still be in your outer spheres of life and especially blessed to be doing date nights with Lisa and Tracy and their hubbies, Mark and Scott! We each prayed for years for our second chance at love and family and got to witness God's miracles for each of us! An excellent mentor to us who took special care of my daughter at Morningside Academy, along with many kind teachers, was Miss Helen Klassen. Dr. Lloyd and Diane Heilman and Scott and Tami Mateer (who created our lovely wedding bouquets and provided elegant flowers to the church and to me) your faithful servanthood is impactful.

Showing up for church, Bible study, and service was utter bliss; all these ladies and their hubbies and many others welcomed us and made us feel like we belonged.

I would not be who I am today without all of my past, and this does include past relationships and painful experiences, especially mistakes made by others and myself. My first marriage is something I remain grateful for because here is where I became a mom, one of life's greatest joys and blessings. I am thankful for the nurturing, love, and life lessons learned from my late mother-in-law. She helped teach me how to be a wife, a mom, and taught me how to bake. She was a loving *Babci* who welcomed any time she could be with her grandbaby. And it is because of this kind, caring, generous woman that my daughter today has close relationships with this side of her family, especially with her *Chauci*. Helping our children keep healthy ties with family members is a good thing and a gift for them for their whole lives. My mother-in-law and I kept in touch with letters and phone calls.

The creative process involves gigantic steps of faith and much collaborative effort with a community of other creatives many times throughout the journey of a creative project. I am full of gratitude for all the hearts who were involved in the shaping of this heart project transformed into this book. My first step of faith toward my writing dreams as an emerging writer occurred in 2009 with WriteByNight founders Justine Tal Goldberg and David Duhr, and again with them and my writing coach Resa Alboher in 2015. The Morningside Church Creative Writers and I, along with eighteen other writers, collaborated and contributed to self-publish *Launching Out, A Collection of Christian Inspirational Stories and Poems* in 2011. Working on this publication put the dream of writing into actual form, which later fed the fires for years afterward toward encouraging my continuous touches on this book. In 2017, I worked with The Writer's

Ally with Allyson E. Machate and participated in Lewis Howes' School of Greatness Academy and was selected for a one-on-one during one of our class sessions. During this session, Lewis suggested changing my memoir genre to non-fiction, and I did. Thanks, Lewis, I'm extremely grateful! Rachelle Gardner and I had a single session of coaching in 2020 where even more insight was beautifully garnered. This book was a dream of the heart since late 1997 and is a reality to behold thanks to brilliant collaboration with the fabulous team at The Fedd Agency. Thank you, Esther, Holly, Brittney, Mariah, Katelyn, and Danielle! Thank you goes to Kyle Negrete, who initially saw something special in my story. Much appreciation to a fellow Jen Hatmaker's *For the Love* book launch team member, Andrea Stunz, who assisted me with reviewing every word, sentence, paragraph. Her editing and feedback were of great value! I am so sweetly grateful to my first readers for their kindness and availability. Having others read your words and memories is a vulnerable, scary process. Scott Beck, Joan Morris Councillor, and Lara Donnell, my heart and project were safe in your hands. Thank you for your perceptive truth.

I am proud to be the daughter of George and Joanna Kijewski, both of whom I admire and love greatly and who shaped and taught me well. Mom went home to Jesus in 2017 and has been missed since. My dad went home to Jesus in January 2024 as this book was in the final editing stages. My creativity, work ethic, and heart are derived from my parents. I received my musical, writing, and love of literature from my mom. Dad passed on his vision, leadership abilities, and passion to achieve, which I remain forever grateful for. I love you, Mom and Dad. Much love to my sisters: Charlene Camillo, who stayed involved in my life and helped me tremendously during my single mom years, including leaving Christmas gifts for us and telling the truth when it came to a certain male acquaintance; and Rachel Kijewski. Rachel is a talented singer, creative, and an activist who has the biggest heart to help I've seen. Joey Kijewski, my extremely intelligent, gifted brother, can figure out anything, had the largest insect collection going, and will always have a special place in my heart. Family, I am thankful for our history and memories together.

When God's promised man, Scott Beck, entered my life, he brought three beautiful young ladies into our lives: Melissa, Jennifer, and Brittany. Jessica was ecstatic that our family was growing, and my heart was looking forward to building relationships with all three girls, who each possessed wonderful qualities and traits.

God has blessed our family with excellent husbands for each of our girls and super dads to our seven grandchildren.

Scott, or Scottie as I call you, thank you for loving me. God has been good to us. I am heart happy with you, my love and best friend. Our courtship was everything my heart ever desired, dreamed of, and prayed for. Our "Boaz"! Thank you for loving my daughter as your own. I love your heart and am privileged to bear witness to your life's journey. You are one of the good ones, sir. You are a great dad and did your best even during your own struggles to heal. You stayed and remained only a call away from each of us. I respect and admire you, Scott Beck. Thank you for honoring boundaries (sugar-free chocolates – LOL) and respecting me. I am looking forward to telling our next story, the story of the mixed blessing after our wedding day and through the blended family acclimation years. I love our many adventures together; I love you and love doing life with you!

The greatest treasure I have received from God is that of being a mom. Dear daughter, you are a gift I value tremendously. I am honored to be your mother and to have had the privilege of watching you grow up from a gorgeous baby to a stunning young woman to a loving wife and mom. I did not always know how to do things and made mistakes, but my love for you never wavered and remains as strong as ever. You and I shared many fun experiences together, and I will cherish our "Jesus, Jessie, and Mommy" years! You have a sweet spirit and creative abilities galore. I love you, sweet, precious daughter! Thank you for being my daughter and loving me!

And the greatest treasure my heart has ever received is Jesus! God, Jesus, and the Holy Spirit are everything for everything! Abba Father, my heart remains forever grateful for your redemption of my soul by sending your Son, Jesus Christ. Jesus, thank you for living on this Earth and dying on the cross for our sins. Your resurrection is an eternal celebration. Holy Spirit, thank you for always helping me. Thank you for rescuing this heart and for loving me and Jessie the way you did and do. Thank you for loving me! Your love transforms. I love our *Junk to Jewels* story, God. A story that continues repeatedly in our lives and is available to any heart who inquires. Inquiries are always desired by your heart.

This book was a labor of absolute love. Through the words written in my journals and prayers unto my Abba Father, it became quite evident my heart desired to share the love God bestowed upon me, a girl who became a woman under God's loving care. During one heartfelt interaction with God, He spoke, clear as day within me, I heard within my heart, *"Daughter, daughter, precious are you. A jewel, fine, one-of-a-kind, sweet, precious, opal."* It was a glorious moment, especially considering I had come from a place of feeling anything but precious, loved, or one-of-a-kind. The words were absorbed into my being, and I knew His truth for me.

Dear readers, you, too, are His precious ones. His opals. His jewels. Each one-of-a-kind. The words within these pages are dedicated to you. May you also discover the love of God—His never-ending love that changes everything. Thank you for walking through my *Junk to Jewels* journey by reading these pages. My highest hope and prayer is that your heart leaves these pages filled with hope and encouragement. May your heart experience a journey from brokenness and despair to beauty and delight!

Resources

Britten, Rhonda, *Change Your Life in 30 Days, A Journey to Finding Your True Self,* 2004, A Perigee

Flanagan, Eileen, *The Wisdom to Know the Difference, When to Make a Change—and When to Let Go*

Harley, Jr., Willard F., *His Needs Her Needs, Making Romantic Love Last*

Jones, D.D., Dennis Merritt, *The Art of Being, 101 Ways to Practice Purpose in Your Life*

Kabat-Zinn, Jon, *Wherever You Go, There You Are, Mindfulness Meditation in Everyday Life*

Kinkade, Thomas, *Simpler Times*

Lehman, Dr. Kevin, *Have a New You by Friday, How to Accept Yourself, Boost Your Confidence & Change Your Life in 5 Days,* 2010, Revell

Lopez, Isabel Rojas', *Parenting from Broken Pieces,* 2018, Stanton Publishing House

Marshall, Catherine, *A Man Called Peter, The Story of Peter Marshall*

McKay, Ph.D., Matthew and Fanning, Patrick, *Self-Esteem, A proven program of cognitive techniques for assessing, improving, and maintaining your self-esteem,* 2000, MJF Books

Meyer, Joyce, *Never Give Up! Relentless Determination to Overcome Life's Challenges,* 2008, Faith Words

Milazzo, Vickie L., *Inside Every Woman, Using the 10 Strengths You Didn't Know You Had to Get the Career and Life You Want Now,* 2006, John Wiley & Sons, Inc.

Moore, Beth, *So Long Insecurity, You've been a bad friend to us*

O'Leary, Jeff, *Footprints in Time, Fulfilling God's Destiny for your Life*

Ortberg, John, *The Life You've Always Wanted, Spiritual Disciplines for Ordinary People*

Prather, Hugh, *Love and Courage,* 2001, Conari Press

Thoele, Sue Patton, *The Courage to be Yourself, A Woman's Guide to Emotional Strength and Self-Esteem,* 2001, MJF Books

Winch, Guy, "How to fix a broken heart," TED, April 2017; https://www.ted.com/talks/guy_winch_how_to_fix_a_broken_heart?utm_campaign=tedspread&utm_medium=referral&utm_source=tedcomshare

Citations

Fisher, H. E., Xu, X., Aron, A., and Brown, L.L. "Intense, Passionate, Romantic Love: A Natural Addiction? How the Fields that Investigate Romance and Substance Abuse Can Inform Each Other." Frontiers in Psychology (2016): 7:687.

"Pinewood." Merriam-Webster.com Dictionary, Merriam-Webster, https://www.merriam-webster.com/dictionary/pinewood. Accessed 18 Jan. 2023.

https://www.spiritualbotany.com/field-notes/the-spiritual-value-of-pine-trees/

https://www.mindfullittleminds.com/family-missionstatement/#:~:text=Why%20create%20a%20family%20mission%20statement%3F%20Having%20a,family%2C%20but%20also%20how%20you%20will%20get%20there.

https://www.worldchallenge.org/davidwilkerson

Why do things get bad before the breakthrough comes? (christiantoday.com)

https://timetogetready.org/miracles/uncomfortable-miracle

http://meanings.crystalsandjewelry.com/opal

https://www.opalauctions.com/learn/opal-information/meaning-of-opal

Friendships: Enrich your life and improve your health; https://www.mayoclinic.org/healthy-lifestyle/adult-health/in-depth/friendships/art-20044860

Genograms: https://www.verywellmind.com/what-is-a-genogram-5217739

Emmanuel, God with Us: https://www.ibelieve.com/faith/the-meaning-and-importance-of-emmanuel-god-with-us.html